"Ka-Ka-Ska-Ska"

("Headwaters to the Gulf – in a kayak)

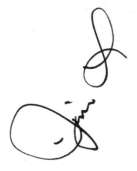

"Ka-Ka-Ska-Ska"

"A man is not old until his regrets take the place of dreams."

-Yiddish proverb

[Dedication]

For Sharron and for her love, patience, and support that only a
spouse can give.

[Acknowledgements]

A successful paddling trip of over 2,300 miles cannot be attributed to any one person or small group. The forty-nine day kayaking adventure down the entire Mississippi River, from the Headwaters to the Gulf of Mexico, took place over the span of three years. The success and safety of this journey was accomplished only as a result of those countless people at home and along the way who supported our efforts with generous acts of good will, kindness and patience. You taught us more about life. I extend a heartfelt thank you to all who helped in any way.

Looking back, I have often wished that I would have done it all in one shot. But then, I know I would not have had the pleasure of paddling with my three companions, (Luke, Andy, and Tony), each one bringing something special to the mix and each one leaving a void when absent. I know that I would never have had the courage to start the journey if it weren't for them.

Thank you to our friends and family who continually cheered us on, especially Sharron, Traci, Chandra, and Niccole. Without them standing behind us, crossing the finish line would never have become a reality.

Thank you to Luke for the idea of dedicating our last seven hundred sixty miles of the journey as a fund raiser for the Relay for Life, American Cancer Society. Also, I wish to thank all those, who in response were so incredibly generous in their giving toward such a worthy cause.

Thank you to special friends and family who spent time proof reading drafts, and were so kind in giving feedback.

Thank you to all who prayed for us. I give glory to God for answering those prayers – for our health, for our safety on

Jim Lewis

and off the water, and for our strength, patience, and endurance along the way.

Thank you to all who are such an integral part of each one of the grand memories.

Jim Lewis,
author

THE RIVER

deep below the surface
deep where no light has ever shown

the source is unknown
its beginnings are hidden

gaining strength with each new day
as a dream that knows no boundaries

left to wander without control
its path determined by what it can consume

defying man's desire to conquer
seemingly nothing will slow its progress

emotions run high along the way
from comfort to fear and back again

those who have made the journey agree
the flow goes on and on to no real end.

Jim Lewis

[In honor of all who battle cancer.]

[Table of Contents]

[2005]

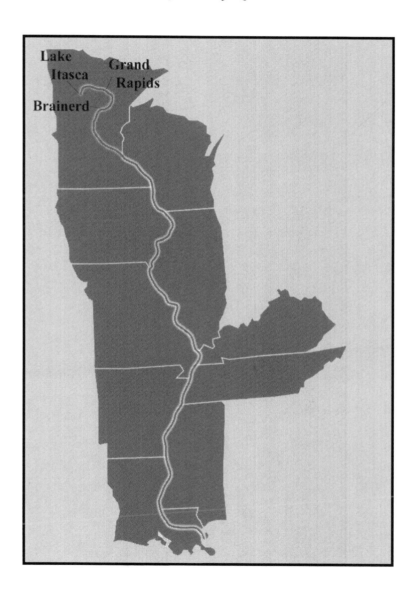

Lake Itasca Grand Rapids Brainerd

[Leg 1]
Headwaters to Bear Den Landing; 34.8 River Miles

Thursday, July 21, 2005

The ninety minute drive across northern Minnesota to the turn off from US Highway 2 onto Beltrami County 5 goes quickly. Another five miles and there's a sign indicating the two vehicles should turn left onto a forest road. A mile or so down the winding sugar-sand single lane is a 'T', and a decision is required; left or right? Without hesitation, I turn left. And Tony, not having experienced any previous consequence of taking my advice, follows blindly. Tony and I then spend what seems to be an eternity (probably closer to the equivalent of watching one episode of *The Jerry Springer Show*) weaving through a network of dusty corrugated trails barely wide enough for the cars. According to the GPS, the elusive Bear Den Landing is on the other side of the planting of the majestic white-pines, but the web of roads doesn't provide a clue as to how to get there. Out of frustration, we return to where the decision was made to go to the left. The road to right leads directly to Bear Den Landing. We'll leave Tony's car here until Sunday afternoon.

"It is also a victory to know when to retreat." -Erno **Paasilinna, essayist and journalist (1935–2000)**

The next stop is Wanagan Landing, the first campsite on the mighty Mississippi River. It is located five river miles from where the Mississippi begins at Lake Itasca, roughly twenty miles southwest of Bemidji, MN. The Minnesota Department of Natural Resources (MN DNR) describes Wanagan Landing as a unique spruce forest, perched above the water table near the point where Sucker Brook runs through Iron Springs Bog Scientific and Natural Area. Sucker Brook supports trout, and enters the Mississippi upstream of the landing.

Though the road leading to Wanagan Landing is much easier to find than Bear Den, it leaves a great deal to be desired. Even to the most casual observer, the more than a mile long track that is not much wider than a car, deserves deliberate and careful restraint of the throttle when ascending and descending the hills where heavy summer rains have left behind cavernous washouts; however, the arduous trek is worth it. The site is much more than expected. It includes a small ten by twelve foot hand scribed log lean-to with a dirt floor, available for whatever your imagination can conjure up. There are both his and hers one-holers, as well as several spacious tent sites, fire rings, and enough dry, split and stacked firewood to satisfy the needs of any self-respecting pyromaniac. If we weren't on a mission, it would be very tempting to camp here more than just overnight.

A local family, who is enjoying a picnic and gathering wild berries, extend a "Howdy." to us upon arrival. It turns out that Grandma, three little girls, and a young mom, are waiting for Grandpa and one of the older kids. They had gone off earlier with a canoe to enter the river at Gulsvig Landing, three miles upstream. After a brief exchange of pleasantries, the tents are set up, and Tony takes a nap in the warm afternoon sun making the best use of time while we wait for Andy and Luke, the other half of this fearless foursome. Andy and Luke left work after we did and will hopefully arrive with the trailer of kayaks soon.

When Grandpa and Older Kid show up in their canoe, I ask about the water level. This is a concern for any river paddler late in the summer when rivers tend to be much lower.

"It's okay. We never had to get out of the canoe once."

"How long did your trip take?"

"Not much more than an hour. It always takes about an hour. We keep a steady pace." As more information is being volunteered, the conversation is interrupted by a thundering rumble easily hitting 90–95 decibels. It's Andy and Luke, and by the sound of it, the muffler on Andy's Honda Civic did not survive the deep ruts in the road.

As we transfer gear and hook up the trailer to my SUV, Grandpa continues to expound on this afternoon's river trip and without any difficulty manages to weave in tales of many jaunts made to Alaska over the years. During his monologue, he interrupts himself at amazingly regular intervals to tell the little girls in the back of his pickup truck, who are joyfully singing camp songs, to "Shut-up". It's painfully apparent that the old man does not have a taste for good music or fun that does not directly involve him.

"The soul is healed by being with children." -Fyodor Dostoyevsky, novelist (1821–1881)

Okay, enough kibitzing with the locals, we're all here and we're going to do it! It has been only nine days since Luke and Andy entered my office to discuss an idea they had come up with over lunch... the bottom line is they want the kayak club to paddle the entire Mississippi River from the Headwaters to the Gulf of Mexico, BUT, not all in one trip. The proposal is to do one section of the river at a time, as work schedules allow.

In less time than it takes to finish a cup of coffee, the decision is made to go ahead even though we don't have a clue as to the length of the Mississippi. It is also evident that no one else has the answer to "How long do you think it is?" either. The site http://en.wikipedia.org/wiki/List of rivers by length reports "The length of a river is hard to calculate. It depends on the identification of the source, the identification of the mouth, and the precise measurement of the river length between source and mouth. As a result, the length measurements of many rivers are only approximations. In particular, there has always been disagreement as to whether the Amazon River or the Nile River is the world's longest river. The source of a river may be hard to determine because a river typically has many tributaries. Among the many sources, the one that is farthest away from the mouth is considered as the source of the river, thus giving a maximal river length. In practice, the tributary with the farthest source is not always the one given the name of the river. For example, the farthest source of the Mississippi River system is the source of the Jefferson River, a tributary of the Missouri River which in turn is a tributary of the Mississippi. However, a different (and shorter) tributary is identified as the Mississippi. When this river is measured from mouth to farthest source, it is called the 'Mississippi-Missouri-Jefferson'. Also, it is hard to state exactly where a river begins, as very often rivers are formed by seasonal streams, swamps, or changing lakes." Yeah. That sounds pretty straightforward.

Well, who are you going to believe? The official tourism site in Minnesota, www.exploreminnesota.com, boasts that the Mississippi is the "world's third largest river." Another site, http://www.ec.gc.ca/WATER/images/nature /prop/a2f3e.htm, states the Mississippi is the second longest river in the world, though ranks sixth in terms of drainage. Then, are you ready for this? The Mississippi doesn't even make the list for the top twenty longest rivers in the world if you check out http://www.vaughns-1-pagers.com/geography/ longest-rivers.htm!

The staff at Itasca State Park located at the Mississippi Headwaters claim the Mississippi is 2,552 miles long. The US Geologic Survey has published a number of 2,300 miles, while the Environmental Protection Agency says it is closer to 2,320 miles long, and the Mississippi National River and Recreation Area maintains its length at 2,350 miles.

Whatever, it's close enough! Whether it's the shortest or the longest river in the universe, it needs to be conquered. The Itasca Kayakers (home office in Grand Rapids, MN – birthplace of Judy Garland) will start at what is perceived to be the beginning of the great waterway, paddle to the end, and come up with a total number of miles on their own.

An email invitation is sent to other club members. Out of nearly seventy kayak paddlers on the distribution list, only four are willing to accept the challenge. At the time the adventure begins...

Jim Lewis – That would be me, the keeper of scrupulous notes and self-proclaimed Czar of the Itasca Kayakers. I have been married for thirty-seven years and I am in my mid-(okay, actually upper)-fifties, a father of three grown children, all girls except for two, and a proud grandfather of four little kids who just happen to be well above average. I have a Master's Degree in Business and currently am employed as a manager in the maintenance department at the local paper mill. I have never owned or driven a power boat, but have loved being on the water since I got my first canoe at age fourteen. Kayaking for me started two years ago. I am the one in the group who usually comes prepared for almost anything. Perhaps it's because of my age and life learned experiences. They (whoever "they" are) say wisdom comes with age; however, others will tell you that in my case it is uncertain if age hasn't shown up all by itself. Though my wife, Sharron, is willing to spend quiet summer afternoons on calm waters, she has been reluctant to participate in any club events involving rivers jammed with fallen trees, portaging across swamps, or sharing personal space with flesh eating flies and/or mosquitoes the size of hummingbirds.

Andy Albertson – At age thirty-one, he and his dog, Buddy, more black lab than his mother (Buddy's mother, not Andy's) co-exist in a charming log home on the Prairie River not far from Buddy's former residence, a cardboard box outside of the Balsam Store. Andy has a degree in Pulp & Paper Science and is employed by the paper mill as an assistant superintendent in operations. Andy owns two kayaks and two sailboats. He is also a very talented wood worker and has produced a number of pieces of fine furniture. Andy earned his Eagle Scout Award at an impressive age of fifteen. Though he enjoys the outdoors, he claims that he would rather drop a bowling ball on any portion of his body rather than ever attempt cross country skiing again. It has something to do with a bad experience in the past.

Luke McLeod – An oddly tall guy, even for his age (twenty-eight), wears size thirteen shoes and lives on Twin Lakes east of Grand Rapids with his wife, Traci, and their three children. Luke has a degree in Pulp & Paper Science and works at the paper mill as a superintendent in operations. He began paddling a canoe when he was eight years old and switched to a kayak four years ago. Luke also enjoys playing poker, golf, fishing, and spending time with family – not necessarily in that order.

Tony Shoberg – The youngest of the group who is barely able to card-in where alcohol is sold is an engineering intern at the paper mill. He will graduate in December of 2005 and has already accepted a job at Bahr Engineering in Duluth. His priorities in life are 1) Kayaking; 1.5) Sleep; 2) Volleyball / Girls – in that order; 3) Eating good food; and 4) Other stuff like camping, family, fishing, making and drinking beer, playing and writing music, biking, cross country and downhill skiing, and travel. It is not certain if it is because of his student status and the lack of a real job or because of his many interests, that Tony does not own a kayak but instead borrows one for each trip. Not having his own boat though, has not stopped him from paddling over 320 miles with the Itasca Kayakers since June of 2004.

"Great geniuses have the shortest biographies." -Ralph Waldo Emerson, writer and philosopher (1803–1882)

Back to today... At the cross roads near the entrance of Itasca State Park, my GPS indicates a need for a right turn. Andy's GPS suggests going farther up the road before making the turn. Luke, thankful for having spent countless hours as a child learning to read actual words and sentences, points to the sign located directly in front of the car. There is an arrow indicating the road to the left is the way to the headwaters.

"... after more than a hundred and fifty years since Marquette and Jolliet had mapped the major portion of the river, a European man came along with enough sense to ask for directions. Henry Schoolcraft asked the Chippewa, OzaWindib, if he knew the location of the river's source. OzaWindib, as Schoolcraft relates, literally pulled out a map and showed him the lake he would later name Itasca. Schoolcraft then asked OzaWindib if he would take him there. The Chippewa agreed and so on July 13, 1832 Henry Schoolcraft became the first European to visit Lake Itasca with the intent of finding the Mississippi's source."[1]

Twenty minutes after Luke's epiphany, still confused and no closer to finding the elusive boat landing, we disembark in a parking lot and follow in Schoolcraft's footsteps. Luke asks for directions (from a guy who happens to be from Ohio, not that that's important). The Ohioan is of no help whatsoever.

"You should be able to get a map from the lodge or find one in town."

"Thanks! [Crap! Where's OzaWindib when you need him?]" We strike out on foot. Sixty yards or so from the parking lot is the small stream of water claimed to be the Headwaters. It's deduced from this that, the boat landing must be on the far side of the lake.

"The world is round and the place which may seem like the end may also be only the beginning." -George Baker (1877–1965)

Be it dumb luck or Devine intervention, we explorer- wannabes finally arrive at the boat landing with a solid two hours of daylight remaining. Like giddy school boys on a fifth grade field trip, the four of us make ready for a journey that countless others only dream of taking.

It requires less than fifteen minutes to paddle the not-quite-a-mile distance across the calm waters to the narrow river channel where we stood earlier. I am the first to negotiate the low dam of small stones that has stood guard at the Lake Itasca outlet since the 1930's. The other three are directly behind me. At an elevation of 1,475 feet above sea level, we enter the Mississippi River.

(Luke crossing dam at Headwaters)

Less than a hundred feet beyond the rock dam, we find ourselves in a stream of water too shallow to float the boats and are forced to exit and drag them downstream for the next mile before the depth is once again adequate. Back in the boats, we paddle through a channel varying from six to ten feet in width. Along the way, three families of mallards are not troubled by the presence of the kayaks and simply swim off to the side allowing the intruders room to pass. Soon, the depth of the channel gives way to shallow waters once again. We are in and out of the boats several more times before reaching Gulsvig Landing, two miles from where we entered the river.

The first lesson learned when paddling a river such as this is that relying on the GPS as a guide to locate the main channel could be a mistake. Clearly, the downloaded GPS maps have not kept up with the constant change of the river's path. It may be hard to imagine but as paddlers we are not sure we have kept up with the changes either, even though we are right here on top of the thing! Evidently, after making a wrong turn we find ourselves having crossed a good-sized beaver pond and are now on the edge of a skillfully knit wall of sticks looking down at least two feet onto the river channel below. Rather than back-track across the four or five acres of water, we swing out toward the center of the pond. Then we turn back to pick up speed, heading directly over the side of the beaver's masterpiece. It is uncertain how the engineers on the project could have antici-pated stress loads of this type. Tony and his boat are the first to test the strength of the dam. It sags only slightly under the combined weight of two hundred-plus pounds. Luke is next, increasing the load by another seventy pounds or so, but the fortification holds tight. Andy and I then line up and take on the wall together, sliding over the top and down the other side back into the river, and yet it remains strong. An eagle perched on the top of a lone dead spruce thirty yards away looks as though he's enjoying the evening's entertainment.

"If an animal does something, we call it instinct; if we do the same thing for the same reason, we call it intelligence."
-Will Cuppy, journalist (1884–1949)

It didn't seem that much time was wasted once on the water but by the time we arrive back at Wanagan Landing, the sun provides scarcely enough light to capture the event on film. Hungry for supper, we don't bother to clean up or change clothes before going back to the state park to retrieve the ve-hicle left there earlier and to find a burger at Lobo's, a nearby watering hole.

Returning to camp at 10:30, a fire is started to dry the wet clothes. It's been a long and exciting day. Tony is the first to go to bed declaring, "It's already three hours past my bedtime." The others follow suit soon after and as everyone settles down in their sleeping bags on the first night of the adventure, the tranquil night air is filled with a soft lullaby from Andy's har-monica.

Friday, July 22, 2005

Two hours after midnight, I am awakened by the sound of light rain tapping out an unfamiliar melody on my tent. I decide to relocate the clothes, drying near the fire, to the protection of the shelter. Before returning to bed, I throw more than a few pieces of wood on the fire in hope of having some hot coals left in the morning. The rain subsides before I drift off back to sleep.

At 5:30, I am the first to get up, and again add more wood to the fire, even though it doesn't need it. Over an hour passes before any other life is seen in the camp. Andy is next to rise, followed by Tony who complains, "This is about three hours earlier than my normal getting-up time when on a day off."

Luke must have forgotten the details of today's plan because there's still no sign of him after yet another hour so Andy and Tony pull the stakes on his tent and make a grand attempt at rolling it over with Luke still inside. The message is sent and received; it's time to at least pretend to be among the living.

Tony had been assigned the task of planning and cooking this morning's breakfast and does a great job on the scrambled eggs, sausage, and hash browns. The only complaint is that there is no orange juice. "I remember buying it, but when I got home, I couldn't find it. I think it must have fallen off the top of my car." Luke suggests that the next time the trunk is full Tony may wish to consider placing any extra items inside the passenger compartment to increase the probability of successful delivery.

"We are all either fools or undiscovered geniuses."
-Bonnie Lin, author

The intent on this end of the river is to keep the boats as light as possible in case there is a need to do any portaging. After eating, camp gear is loaded into my SUV. Andy and I will shuffle it to Coffee Pot Landing fifteen river miles downstream where we'll break for lunch. By no means do we rush into this operation, so the kayaks don't get on the river until after ten.

As a matter of fact, considering what lies ahead, the morning is actually pretty relaxed with no sense of hurry-let's-get-going. There is no discussion regarding personal thoughts and true feelings, but each one of us macho-men is more than aware that we are on the brink of one of the greatest adventures of our lives. Time spent here in this spot will never be duplicated; it is a time to relax and reflect. Besides, it's a day away from work with an incredible backdrop. There's a warm morning sun rising slowly in a sky without clouds. A gentle breeze whispers through the towering white pine. Spirited little chipmunks and birds filled with curiosity flitter about, questioning the intrusion into their world.

"It is better to have loafed and lost than never to have loafed at all." -James Thurber, writer and cartoonist (1894–1961)

The paddling begins this morning on a narrow stream of water with almost no flow. It continues through marsh land for almost six miles before shifting to higher ground and some faster water near Vekin's Dam. The wooden dam was built in the early 1900s to assist with moving logs down river and creates a four to five foot drop over the next twenty-five yards. The upstream approach to the dam is somewhat clogged with a couple of smaller trees and brush floating in the river. This prevents us from being able to build up speed needed to slide over the dam. According to the map, there is a fifty yard portage on river-left. However, time is not to be spent portaging if it can be avoided, so one by one we take on the challenge. The kayaks handle the initial two and a half foot drop without too much trouble except for my Perception Captiva which is the longest at fifteen and a half feet. It gets hung up on the stern causing a brief but very precarious situation that could have turned out much differently without some welcomed assistance from Luke.

(Andy slipping over the drop)

Trees come with higher ground. Trees that grow too close to the river bank for their own good and often times end up crosswise the channel. The number of dead falls, or what are sometimes referred to as strainers, is minimal over the next four to five miles compared to what the Itasca Kayakers have come up against on other northern Minnesota rivers in the past. Only once in this stretch of the Mississippi are we forced to portage.

The high ground and sandy river bottom continues to fade in and out of marsh. Along the way, near the shoreline, there is a clay formation slightly below the surface that is perhaps three feet in diameter looking like a mockup of a small volcano. The spring, or whatever constant force from below, pushes the clay upward and out into the river. For almost a mile, the water is clouded to the point where the paddles disappear as soon as they dip below the surface. Regrettably, a picture of this phenomenon is not taken. [We find out later from a geologist friend, Katie Heimgartner, this is quite natural and is simply called a mud volcano or soft sediment defamation.]

As we paddle through the marsh and swampy areas, we again find it difficult to trust the GPS to keep us on the channel. It is generally safer to watch the grasses on the river bottom to see which direction they have been coerced, and try to follow the flow in that manner. But when the flow is slow, the grasses fail to provide much of a clue. At a fork in the river, Andy makes the decision to go right. I lead Tony and Luke in the opposite direction. The channel of river through the bulrushes I take them down soon gets so narrow that we can no longer continue nor turn around. Luke who is at the tail end of the pack comes to the rescue. He exits his boat into the waist deep water and a mucky bottom to pull us back to where we had turned.

Averaging less than 4 mph, we arrive at Coffee Pot Landing four hours from the time we got on the river. We think this is decent progress but in reality have nothing to compare it to.

Lunch consisting of bagel sandwiches, chips, and droopy granola bars washed down with PowerAde is not rushed. Entertainment is provided by another Grandpa (AKA Grandpa-2) and three kids. Kid-1, a seven-year-old, is first seen across the river in the parking lot. He has a crawfish in the bottom of a five gallon bucket filled to the brim with water and asks for help to carry it down the hill. Andy suggests he pour out some of the water so it would be lighter, and then refill it when he gets to the river. Even though Kid-1 takes Andy's advice, Tony helps him carry the bucket anyway. Kid-2, who looks like he's maybe three years older than Kid-1, connects with Andy down by the river, where he is trying to catch his own crawfish. Andy says Kid-2 reminds him of a boy he knew in grade school who for no apparent reason would get beat up from time to time. Kid-3, a delightful little girl about age six, wanders over to say hello but is unwilling to share her ice cream. Grandpa-2 is totally into this time with family. Other than stopping to take our picture when asked, he is focused on playing with the kids and snorkeling in the shallow river looking for treasures to share with his little charges.

*"Happiness? It is an illusion to think that more comfort means more happiness. Happiness comes of the capacity to feel deeply, to enjoy simply, to think freely, to risk life, to be needed." -*Unknown

After lunch, while we are getting our life jackets on, Luke is suddenly aware of a half-dozen leeches that have attached themselves to his body in a variety of places; most likely a result of being in the murky water earlier. It seems that he is not at all comfortable with this situation, and erupts into some amazing gyrations. Minutes later, free of the leeches, (without any help from those standing nearby) Luke tries to be as careful as he can be not to come in contact with the water while getting in his boat. Not careful enough though. His boat proves to be much more raring to go than he is and without warning, it slides out from under him. Luke's first words as his head comes up out of the water are, "This better not show up in the journal!"

The next three-plus miles are extremely difficult due to frequent hairpin turns in a waterway that is often times not much wider than the kayaks. There is little or no chance to get up any speed before having to stop and make a turn. It's hard work and the sun is hot with the temperature in the upper seventies. I call for a break at the approach to Stumphges Rapids but the break is cut short when Tony suggests we push on and look for a place to swim. The swimming never happens.

Almost twenty miles from last night's campsite, I zoom out and pan the GPS screen looking for opportunities to cut through weeds and cattails in hope of shaving off some distance. More successful than not, the extra effort spent crossing through the heavy foliage is still easier than paddling the "open water." The absolute worst alternate route is less than two miles from the take-out, when I convince the other three to push through a spot that looks to be about two hundred feet in depth. This would shorten the overall paddle by at least four times that much. Ground is lost on this move. Every inch is a struggle.

(Tony in the lead)

"Ka-Ka-Ska-Ska"

There is virtually no water at all, making it necessary to reach out with both hands, grab a handful of weeds and pull both yourself and your kayak forward a few inches. Then, repeat the process again and again to cross the field of bulrushes. Tony is in the lead followed by me, then Luke, then Andy. Somewhere around halfway through the thicket, I lose track of my paddle. As I pull on the cattails to move ahead, my paddle evidently slipped backwards off the top of my boat. I am confident that I notice its absence almost immediately, but there is no sign of the paddle anywhere. Luke is directly behind me and claims he did not see it though I am not sure if Luke is being completely honest. To prove his innocence, Luke manages to get out of his boat and while standing in the muck (evidently having forgotten about the earlier encounter with leeches) he rolls his kayak up on its side to see if somehow my paddle managed to get underneath. It's not there! By now, I am on the edge of a possible meltdown, thinking that my new $150 paddle has been sucked to the depths by the great river gods and will never be seen again. A moment before the pressure gauge is about to blow, Luke confesses. The paddle didn't just happen to slide off my boat. Luke saw opportunity and with a quick hand grabbed it and passed it back to Andy for him to hide. You can't trust anyone, even in the middle of the wilderness.

"There is only one way to achieve happiness on this terrestrial ball, and that is to have either a clear conscience or none at all." -Ogden Nash, author (1902–1971)

It's nearing twilight when we arrive at Bear Den Landing, logging in not quite thirty miles for the day, averaging well under 3 mph. Now we have to retrieve the other cars left and get something to eat before going home. Everyone is tired and doesn't hesitate to admit the trip was far more difficult than anticipated, but not so difficult that giving up should be a consideration. Failure is not an option.

We all have other plans on our calendars for the rest of the weekend so it will be at least a couple of weeks before returning – but we're proud to have taken the first step toward completing the voyage to the Gulf of Mexico.

Trip Report
- — 34.8 miles completed (1.5% of total trip)
- — 2,272.2 to The Gulf

[Leg 2]

Bear Den Landing to Knutson Dam;
54.7 River Miles

Thursday, August 11, 2005

Andy, Tony, and I leave Grand Rapids after work at three in the afternoon. Again two vehicles are taken. One will be dropped at the Iron Bridge campsite before going on to the put-in at Bear Den Landing. Luke can't make the trip at this time and will have to do a make up session on his own. Two other club members are getting on the band wagon though. Brian Hanson will drive up later today and meet us at Iron Bridge. And Joan Bibeau is planning to connect with the group at the lunch break tomorrow. Neither Brian nor Joan had initially indicated that they wanted to start at the Headwaters, but probably changed their minds after hearing how much fun was had.

On the way to the put-in, we stop at the Cass Lake Dairy Queen after an hour of driving to get something to eat. It surprises us that the DQ does not accept credit cards. Otherwise we may have considered bringing more than $2.00 in cash.

Andy asks the high school girl behind the counter, "Would you accept a third-party, out-of-state check, that is no good?"

"I think it would be okay, but I have to check with my manager first. Okay?"

Andy confesses that he has a real checking account with real money. The burgers are ordered to go and little time is frittered away before getting back on the road.

At the turn off for the Iron Bridge Campsite, we are baffled because the road to the campsite shown on the county map, the GPS, and the aerial photos found online before leaving the office is nothing more than a private drive. We consult the little side notes on the MN DNR river map once more and discover a hint to solving the dilemma. "The [Iron Bridge] campsite is accessible by river only." How were we to know? The DNR was called prior to the last outing in regard to the access to the Wanagan Landing. The ranger said it would be almost impossible to get down with a car and furthermore, a four-wheel drive pulling a trailer would not be advisable either. We proved that was not the case at all. It was quite doable. Andy's muffler would have probably fallen off anyway.

That was then. This is now, and obviously the plan that's in place isn't going to work. After minimal debate, it is decided to leave Andy's car along with the camp gear at Iron Bridge Landing. It is located next to the highway and only a half-mile downstream from the campsite. We'll go ahead and get on the river at Bear Den Landing, (site of the last take-out), paddle down the fourteen miles, have Brian meet us here, and then head over to Pine Point Campsite for the night. That probably sounds more confusing than it really is, and to the reader doesn't mean anything. To us, it means more shuffling of cars. The trade-off is that we won't have to pack the gear in the boats and paddle upstream after Brian's arrival later.

It is close to 6:00 when we arrive at Bear Den Landing, with ample paddle time remaining before the sun sets. While Tony and I unload the boats, Andy says he'll be right back and disappears into the forest. When he returns, he shares a new lesson learned, "Always check the area for man-eating ants BEFORE sitting down in the woods for any reason."

"What matters is not the idea a man holds, but the depth at which he holds it." -Ezra Pound, poet (1885–1972)

The boats are in the water and the wildlife is abundant — herons, two otter, a small beaver, and plenty of ducks. Seeing the ducks prompts Tony to tell the story of when he was five years old and visiting his uncle's house which was on a lake. Tony spotted some ducks swimming near the end of the dock. He found a small rock and threw it, "…just to scare 'em." The rock does more than scare them. It hit one of the ducks in the head and killed it. Tony ran up to the house, crying, "I tipped over a duck!" His uncle, probably trying to encourage more of this type of behavior, retrieved the duck and served it up for supper.

"We all love animals; why do we call some pets and others dinner?" -K.D. Lang, singer (1961–)

The focus on getting to where we have to go is lost after only two miles of paddling. We begin to take short cuts and play hide-and-seek in the marshy wetland, taking turns being the one who is 'it' all the while slowly working our way down the river. The game continues for an hour or so until Andy finds himself hung up on a bog when going into hiding. He didn't only need to be found, but needed to be rescued. It's time to get serious.

Within a few hundred yards, the river channel disappears and in another hour, the sun will too. We have entered a portion of the Mississippi that according to the MN DNR map (that was left behind in the car)… "The river meanders though a large wetland from this point to Iron Bridge Landing. Bog chunks can become dislodged and float downstream. This can be a navigational hazard. This condition is not dangerous, but it is advisable to call the regional DNR office to determine conditions before planning the trip." It sure would have been wise to have taken time to read this little tidbit of information prior to getting on this stretch of water – without any camp gear.

Not knowing the magnitude of this situation, we are confident that we can find a passage through or over the bog. Each one of us goes off on our own to find the best route. The marsh grasses and bulrushes range from six to seven feet tall, limiting visibility to no farther than the front of the boat. At first, a lot of headway is gained – perhaps a mile or so. It's tough going, but at least we're going. Then I become stuck! I have pulled myself through a portion of the bog to a point of no return. My boat will not go forward nor back, not even an inch. After my repeated calls for help, Andy responds and somehow works his way through the labyrinth to locate the track I had left behind. With Andy on the scene, I feel more comfortable getting out of my boat to stand on the "bog stumps." If I can balance on the floating clumps of mud and grass, and at the same time lift my boat, I may be able to get it turned around.

"The diligent find freedom in their work..." -**Proverbs 12:24, The Message**

The first remnant of bog where I am standing begins to sink, motivating me to move to a new location and continue to lift and rotate my boat from there. Three or four inches at a time in a radial direction is considered good progress, though each negligible increment comes only after a major struggle. Andy can only provide encouragement as he sits and watches. The thought is to get the almost sixteen foot craft turned far enough where I can get a rope on the bow, then have Andy grab on the other end of the rope and pull during the lifting process. After repeatedly moving from one sinking bog stump to the next, lifting and pulling, while flattening any cattails and swamp brush getting in the way, the boat is eventually back in the water pointing in the opposite direction. Just in time too, because the sun is resting at the top of the tree line – but not for long and I am running out of clumps of mire and grass for support. Simply standing on the bottom of the river is not an option. When checked, my 230cm paddle was too short to measure the actual depth of the water and mud.

In the mean time, Tony has gone in search of a way to get to shore. He reports back as the bog debacle comes to an end. "There is a trail of open water that will get us within a hundred yards of high ground along the north shore."

Andy checks his GPS and locates a forest trail running parallel to the river; the new objective. When we arrive at the edge of the quagmire protecting the high ground, we use our kayaks like giant boots placing one foot in the cockpit, and the other strategically on bog stumps along the way. We lean into it, limping and sliding toward dry land.

Darkness greets us on shore, but at least we have made it safely off the river, after having paddled a mere six miles since our put-in. The location where the boats are abandoned is marked on the GPS and only the essentials are taken: a beverage, cell phones, cameras, flashlights, and of course the GPS. It's agreed not to make another attempt at the remaining eight miles of river between here and Iron Bridge Landing – not even in daylight.

The forest trail is exactly where it is supposed to be, and we river travelers are about seven miles (by road) from where we are supposed to be. It would make a nice stroll, but instead Andy gives Brian a call to see if he can come pick us up.

"Not a problem." He is about to leave Bemidji which is fifteen miles away.

The cell signal is poor at best and there is a concern that Brian was not able to hear the directions. We begin to walk, so at least we are doing something, even if it is only to make us feel good. After a few minutes, Andy suggests we slow down, "I don't think it's necessary to walk too fast. Brian has a car capable of going faster than 60 mph, so the little distance we gain toward him will be meaningless."

"It is an ironic habit of human beings to run faster when we have lost our way." -Rollo May, psychologist (1909–1994)

We walk on, perhaps a half mile down the road. Near a farmhouse, we evidently disturb a couple of hypersensitive watch dogs possessing if nothing else, seemingly life-threatening barks. Fortunately for us vagrants, that is all the dogs have going for them, and they do not exhibit any other fervent behavior.

We walk on. At least another mile of road is now at the rear. Tony hears a noise off to the side. He aims his flashlight in that direction catching the reflection of a pair of cold slime-green eyes belonging to an inquisitive brush wolf standing in the tall grass on the far side of the ditch. No sooner than being caught in the beam of light, the wolf turns and trots away, disappointed to discover that what he had been scoping out was not the venison he'd hoped for.

We walk on. With less than four miles of dark country road remaining between us and Iron Bridge Landing, there is still no sign of Brian. Andy tries calling again, but is only able to leave a message on Brian's voicemail. It seems much more than an hour since leaving the boats. Up ahead, a car's headlights shine over the rise. A minute later, the car stops. Yes! It's Brian! He claims he has been on every back road west of Bemidji at least once. Everyone is thankful for his perseverance.

Arriving back at Iron Bridge Landing, we split up. Tony and Andy drive to Pine Point Landing to set up camp. Brian and I go back to Bear Den Landing to get my vehicle and the trailer.

Brian and I arrive at Pine Point Landing well after the other two. We discover that Tony and Andy had, in the meantime, dropped in on the neighbors at the next campsite, beer-drinking teenagers with loud music. The kids were so glad that Tony and Andy weren't the law that they gave them each a cold beer. Neither Tony nor Andy, however, had any recollection that they were traveling with two other people who could possibly be thirsty too.

A bit past midnight of another long day, we finish off our supper of soup, lunch meat, and chips. Tony takes time to tie the trash bag containing the empty soup cans on the high overhang of the shelter as we unwind, telling and retelling of the evening's adventure.

"I don't know why we are here, but I'm pretty sure that it is not in order to enjoy ourselves." -Ludwig Wittgenstein, philosopher (1889–1951)

Friday, August 12, 2005

I am the first to look outside of my tent at the same time the sun is making its debut for the day. The campground is quite impressive in the daylight. The tent sites are spread across two or three acres of trimmed grass amongst many large pines. Again, there is an ample supply of firewood.

Less than an hour later, Brian is the next one to greet the new day. He and I heap pine branches onto the fire believing the crackling of the flames and smoke-filled air will awaken the other two. The scheme works well and the camp begins to come alive. As Tony emerges, I compliment him on how well the tactic of hanging the trash up high worked. "There was no way bears, raccoons, skunks, or any other varmints bent on creating havoc were going to reach it."

"Thanks. It was a good thing too. Otherwise there would have been two empty cans all over the place."

When Andy is ready, he and I leave to retrieve the boats that had been left to fend for themselves in the wilderness overnight. Using the four-wheel drive, we are able to get relatively close, although we still have to drag them fifty yards through the woods from where they had been concealed.

Back at camp two hours later, Brian is out for his morning run after having already completed a ten mile bike ride. Brian, a twenty-six year old construction electrician, stands five foot-fifteen inches tall and weighs in at a hundred-seventy pounds. He and his dog, a German shorthair who responds to the name Rusty, live in Chisholm, MN forty miles northeast of Grand Rapids. Brian's passion for physical fitness has driven him to compete in Adventure Duluth twice. Adventure Duluth is a full day of competition including a mile of swimming; kayaking nine miles; mountain biking eighteen miles; in-line skating on a rolling course slightly more than twelve miles long; white water canoeing a four mile stretch of wild river; and then finishing with a ten mile trail run. More often than not, people enter as part of a team. This is not the case for Brian who competes as a solo entrant. Brian has also run Grandma's Marathon in Duluth three times and competed three times in the Wisconsin American Berkebeiner, a thirty-one mile cross country ski race, plus a number of lesser known triathlons. In 2004, Brian was a participant in the Iowa Half-Iron Man competition, and is planning to do the Full Iron Man in 2006. The Full Iron Man competition begins with nearly two and a half miles of swimming, followed immediately with a hundred and twelve miles of biking, and then a brisk twenty-six mile jog, all of which has to be completed before sun-down. Once, while on vacation in British Columbia, Brian spent time cross country skiing with the U.S. Olympic Team. Actually, the O Team was skiing on the same mountain during the day and drinking in the same bar at night.

"The only person you should ever compete with is yourself. You can't hope for a fairer match." -Todd Ruthman

Tony is cooking French toast and bacon this morning. Orange juice is also on the table. (Evidently he heeded Luke's advice regarding what to do with extra items when the trunk is full.) Tony wants to know, "Whose sock is on the picnic table?"

Andy, "That would be mine."

"Can I use it as a pot holder?"

"Sure. But I need it back because it's part of today's wardrobe."

We don't leave for the put-in at Iron Bridge Landing until eleven. Once there, Tony and I will stay behind to get the boats

ready. Andy and Brian will go on to drop a car at the County 11 Bridge, where we will have a late lunch and connect with Joan Bibeau.

Joan is the club's newest member. She began paddling a canoe as a teenager and purchased her first kayak a week ago. She has her master's degree in Elementary Education and is probably best described as a teacher's teacher. In 1997, Joan was recognized by the Northeastern Minnesota Citizens League Equity in Education for her work relating to equality for an early childhood program for all children in the community. In 2005, the Minnesota Indian Education Association named Joan as the Outstanding American Indian Teacher of the Year. She is also quite the gardener and enjoys cooking – but absolutely no meat! As a matter of fact, Joan prides herself on eating only natural foods. (Evidently she, like so many others sharing the same eating habits, has yet to hear that millions of people die every year of natural causes.)

Upon arriving at Iron Bridge Landing, I check my GPS. Almost one hundred miles has been driven since putting in at Bear Den Landing last evening; however, only six miles has been paddled. The miles driven were logged in retrieving the boats and moving my vehicle down river. The roads in this area do not go where paddlers need them to go, and there are very few locations where bridges cross the river.

It is noon before the paddling commences, and once on the river, there is more wildlife. Dozens of Canada Geese and a variety of ducks are readying for their own trip south. A deer swimming across the river a few yards downstream in front of the kayaks is seemingly oblivious to our presence.

"Ka-Ka-Ska-Ska"

This section of the river is narrow, not much more than thirty feet across in many places. The moderate flow through this high ground yields to frequent deadfalls that easily stretch from one bank to the other. Most of the fallen trees are passable, either over the top or underneath. There are only two rather large oaks that leave no other option but for us to portage.

It's twelve-plus miles of river to County 11 Bridge. We arrive at 3:00, minutes after Joan. The approach guardrails up on the highway serve as a picnic table. After a quick sandwich, Brian, Andy, and I leave to relocate the vehicles from Iron Bridge Landing to the next take-out at the Ottertail Power Co. Dam. The logistics of leap-frogging on a river trip is never straight-forward and, more often than not, a lot easier said than done.

When Brian, Andy, and I get to the dam to leave a car, we find no easy river access, so Plan-B is unveiled. The MN DNR map indicates a boat landing on Stump Lake. After a great deal of searching for the Stump Lake Access, however, we find ourselves on private land and for the third time, backing out of the same driveway. That's when the land owner appears. Andy asks him about the boat landing. "It was shut down about ten years ago." Plan-C: Park the take-out vehicle at the bridge along the road on the east side of Lake Bemidji on County 19 and take Andy's car back to County 11 Bridge.

"Don't find fault. Find a solution." -Henry Ford, U.S. industrialist and automobile manufacturer (1863–1947)

Back at County 11 Bridge, Tony and Joan have two completely different stories of what took place in our absence.

Tony's story... "I'm taking a nap when I hear this car pull up that sounds like it needs more than minor work on the exhaust system. At first, I think it's Andy's car. Then I look up, and I see this guy with long, greasy hair who looks like he's going to steal our stuff. I think he spotted the cooler here by the road, but didn't see me lying in the ditch taking a nap, so he dynamites the brakes and hops out. As soon as I raise my head, he starts picking flowers."

Joan's story... "It was so cool. A love-struck Latino stopped. He was on his way to see his girlfriend when he eyes a patch of wild flowers right here beside the guardrail. He was so excited that he turned around in the middle of the road and came back for them. I helped him pick some and arrange a bouquet for his girl friend."

Note to reader... It's your call.

Returning to the water at 5:00, the first half mile is tough going due to more trees across the river. After that, the river widens and paddling is easier for a few minutes. Things change though when the river enters Lake Irving and passes through Lake Bemidji. We take a heading of north by northeast toward the exit channel three miles away while the 16–18 mph west wind manages to stir up an offensive of whitecaps. The scrimmage with the rough water takes well over an hour.

Arriving at County 19 after the four mile paddle, there's still enough daylight to make one more shuffle. Though we were unable to find a parking place near the Ottertail Power Co. Dam earlier, the thought is now to park farther away on the ATV trail, a half-mile to the west. Andy says it is good to have Brian, the marathon runner, along today. When we land later, it will most likely be on private property and Brian can run to get the vehicle so we can make a fast exit. Andy thinks this is a good use of the ability to run, "Normally the only opportunity where running is practical is to get through rain or to catch a bus."

"We can't solve problems by using the same kind of thinking we used when we created them." -Albert Einstein, physicist, Nobel laureate (1879–1955)

The paddle continues another six miles. While we are crossing Stump Lake, the sun sets, the wind becomes still, and the kayaks slice effortlessly across the flat water in the waning light as the loons present each other with a "Good night." After not quite twenty-two miles of paddling since Iron Bridge, a conveniently placed dock in a small backwater that is close to both the dam and the highway becomes the final take-out. (Never mind the NO TRESPASSING sign painted in big red letters)

On the way back to get the other cars, the decision is made to paddle again tomorrow. But tonight we will go home and sleep in our own beds. It's 12:30 A.M., when we arrive in Grand Rapids.

Sunday, August 14, 2005

The weather is too good to pass up the opportunity to continue on with Leg 2. Andy, Tony, Joan, and I fuel up two vehicles at the Grand Rapids M&H and drive the hour to Knutson Dam boat ramp which is going to be the take-out point for today. Andy's car is left behind, and the trailer is transferred to my SUV.

Another hour and the boats are unloaded on the downstream side of Ottertail Power Co. Dam next to the bridge.

There's a narrow walking trail that serpentines through tall grass down the hillside to the river. To the right of the trail is a much steeper section of grassy hillside. It is at least a forty-five degree incline stretching to a fifty-plus foot elevation above the river. Adjacent to the grass slope are thickets of brush and a scattering of numerous rocks up to a foot in diameter. At the bottom of this descent are a few small maples and oaks.

Time is not to be wasted by walking down to the river to check out what can't be seen from the top of the hill. Tony enters the cockpit of his (actually Luke's) kayak and pushes off down the trail. The Jamaican bobsled team has nothing on Tony, as his kayak sticks to the trail like a marble in a trough all the way to the river! "Piece of cake," he calls back from below.

Andy's turn is next. He manages to stay on the trail for about as long as a "Yee-Haa", then his boat opts for the shortest distance between two points. Out of control, his kayak veers off the edge of trail and straight down the steeper portion of the hill bouncing over rocks and through the brush, somehow managing to miss the larger trees. Even more amazing is that Andy is able to maintain a death grip on his paddle during the harrowing ride, and makes it into the river right side up. Joan and I are quick studies, and take the more conventional approach. We walk down the trail, dragging our boats behind us. It's not as fast.

"The mark of the immature man is that he wants to die nobly for a cause, while the mark of a mature man is that he wants to live humbly for one." -Wilhelm Stekel, physician and psychologist (1868–1940)

The water level for the first two miles of the river below the dam isn't even a foot deep in most places, calling for more paddling effort than had been counted on. It is still better than the narrow winding water trace through the swamps encountered nearer the Headwaters. As the kayaks slide along through the water, fish swimming in the shallows are startled, but the herons, eagles, and ducks along the shoreline show little concern for us travellers. The sky is a gorgeous deep summer blue, the temp is nearing seventy, and there's a slight breeze rustling through the leaves of the hardwoods lining the riverbanks. It's a day that spurs memories of carefree youth when you were allowed to run free and do only the things you wanted to do – to explore the wilds of neighboring forests and daydream of forbidden adventures.

The river gets deeper and paddling easier after traversing a short Class I rapids a half-mile beyond Island Point Campsite, but that doesn't mean going any faster. Today is Sunday and it's a time to relax and enjoy.

At a place called High Banks, five miles downstream from this morning's put-in, there is an incredibly steep sand hill on the north side of the river. Tony stops on shore after very little coaxing. With nothing less than a major struggle, he drags the sixty-five pounds of boat up as far as he can, but yet is only a fourth of the way to the top. He then gets back in and slides down toward the river. One would think with a hill that steep, sliding too fast would be the concern. It is not. Instead, the speed down the hill is not much faster than the trip up. When Tony eventually gets to the water, only the front half the boat makes it into the river, leaving the back of the boat hung up on the beach teetering until Andy paddles over to save him.

After the rescue, Andy says, "Okay. What did we learn from this exercise?"

"The coefficient of friction of sand is different than that of damp grass."

"He should have gone up higher."

Both are valid points to be entered into the 'what-did-we-learn' database.

Shortly after noon, the crossing of Wolf Lake begins with a tailwind of 16 mph (I have an anemometer). Andy doesn't let this opportunity pass by, and fashions a sail using his rain coat. He is able to get up to 3.9 mph.

Lake Andrusia is next. A tandem kayak is on the lake ahead of us, but turns to the north as we go toward the river's outlet in the southeast. The two in the "divorce boat" probably don't even realize they weren't alone on the lake.

At the County Rd 33 Bridge, someone has stencilled "Ben Stinks" on the side of the structure. We take it as fact, because it is the fifth bridge with the same bit of constructive criticism since leaving Lake Itasca.

"If you devote your life to seeking revenge, first dig two graves." -Confucius, philosopher and teacher (c. 551–478 BCE)

The wind ramps to 20 mph as we begin the trek across Cass Lake, allowing Andy to use his rain coat more than his paddle. Cass Lake is named for Lewis Cass, who as governor of Michigan sought the Mississippi's Headwaters in 1820. He ended his journey at this lake, then known as Red Cedar Lake for the trees that dominated its shorelines. Henry Schoolcraft travelled with Cass in 1820 and vowed to reach the river's Headwaters. He renamed the lake when he concluded the trip in 1832.

"Ka-Ka-Ska-Ska"

A little more than three miles from where we entered Cass Lake, we stop at Star Island for lunch. Once the home of the Ojibwe, this is the largest of four islands on the lake. It has over eight miles of shoreline and six miles of hiking trails. There is also a lake on the island; Windigo Lake. In the television series *Ripley's Believe It Or Not*, the lake was designated as being the only lake within a lake in the Northern Hemisphere. (There are actually a few other such lakes.)

The lake derives its name from the windigo ceremony of the Ojibwe people. A windigo (or Wendigo) was a malevolent, cannibalistic spirit that could possess people and inspire cannibalism. Windigo ceremonies were often performed during times of famine as a reminder to be wary of the windigo spirits. The last known windigo ceremony in the United States was to have taken place on Star Island, thus the lake was named Windigo. [2]

On today's lunch menu, we have bagel sandwiches enhanced with home grown tomatoes from Joan's garden. She also brought fresh radishes, cucumbers, pickles, and tempeh (hippie term for soybeans cooked in soy sauce). The fresh vegetables are a good treat and disappear quickly though there is a lot of leftover tempeh.

Shortly after 4:00, we are back in the boats, ready to cross the last four miles of open water. The wind remains strong at our backs for maybe a mile or so, as we head straight east. When we are passing O'Neil's Point the wind shifts to the southwest. Most of the waves range from one to three feet, forcing Andy to give up on his sail, even though he's able to reach 6.0 mph. Then he, along with Tony and I surf some of the larger waves. While surfing without the sail, Andy's GPS locks in at 9.1 mph.

Two miles to go before the take-out, Andy is to my left and slightly behind me when he catches a colossal wave and begins the surf. Andy immediately closes the gap on me, and as the same wave starts to lift my boat, I dig my paddle in for the ride. Whether it's the wind, the stroke of the paddle, or whatever, my boat is lifted up on the apex of the wave and swung instantaneously ninety degrees to the left; directly over the top of Andy's boat in the swell. I shout a warning and Andy ducks forward in his cockpit just in time to escape being hit in the head with the hull of my boat. With a good five to six feet of the front of my boat suspended out of the water over Andy, and in response to the shortest prayer known to man, "Oh God!", Andy's entire boat passes beneath mine without a collision.

"I'm gonna pray now; anyone want anything?" -Flip Wilson, comedian (1933–1998)

The day ends at Knutson Dam at 5:30 P.M. after having paddled over eighteen fun miles.

Trip Report
- 89.5 miles completed (3.9% of total trip)
- 2,217.5 to The Gulf

[Leg 2]
SUPPLEMENT

Thursday, August 18, 2005

It's mid-morning when the charter flight lands at the Grand Rapids Airport in near zero visibility amidst a drenching rain and east winds at twenty-five per. The prediction for the rest of the day: "The rain will taper off by early afternoon with cloud cover remaining. Severe thunderstorms are likely for this evening, ending around midnight."

As the plane taxies to the hanger, Luke tells his co-workers/traveling companions that he needs to do some catch-up in the office. And then he plans to go paddling on the Mississippi to make up for the section of river missed last weekend. When asked how far he plans to paddle, he responds, "Those %$!@&&$ * [cherished friends] paddled over forty miles. Now I have to do the same!"

Over lunch, Luke rushes home to pack his gear: boat, paddle, tent, sleeping bag, spare shirt, and rain coat. Logistics are worked out with me later in the afternoon. As soon as Luke is able to leave work, both he and I will drive to the take-out at Knutson Dam. At that point, Luke's boat will be transferred to my vehicle. The two of us will ride together to the put-in at Iron Bridge Landing. There, Luke will set sail and I will return home.

We leave Grand Rapids not quite two hours later than planned. Oh well. Luke's car is dropped off at the Dam, and the next stop is the Cass Lake Super Valu. I wait in the parking lot while Luke runs in to "get some bare necessities."

This turns into more than a five minute pit stop. Luke eventually returns with two bags of groceries and a chicken dinner for tonight's supper. Items purchased for this little overnight outing on the river include a family-size box of Wheat Thins, a large package of pepperoni, sliced mozzarella cheese, string cheese, several bananas, a family-size bag of peanut M&M's, six breakfast bars, and eight thirty-two ounce bottles of PowerAde. I'm not sure if this is a case of: "Never go into a grocery store on an empty stomach." or "Always be prepared."

"Society is composed of two great classes: those who have more dinners than appetite, and those who have more appetite than dinners." -Sebastien-Roch-Nicolas de Chamfort, writer (1741–1794)

Arriving at Iron Bridge Landing, Luke steps off into the woods to change clothes. A new lesson learned. "When in the woods, always check the area BEFORE you lay down the clothes you are removing. And, be on the alert for such things as toilet paper; especially used toilet paper."

Enlightened with that touch of new knowledge, Luke launches his kayak as I share the latest forecast. "Another front is moving in from the west, and they're talking about serious storms including possible tornados. But! There's a chance they may split off and head to Canada. So, have fun and be careful!"

Psyched for the trip, Luke thinks to himself, *"This won't be a big deal. I'll paddle for an hour or so, and then set up camp when it gets dark."*

All is going well. Luke has traveled over four miles in his first hour. While paddling this first stretch, the art of mind games begin. *"Drinks of PowerAde will only be permitted every hour, and only if a minimum of four miles are paddled during the hour. No more than one minute will be allowed for each break."* His first break lasts roughly ten seconds, then it's back to paddling.

Another hour passes and another less-than-a-minute break is awarded. No rain yet, and there is still thirty minutes of dim twilight remaining before there will be a need for a headlamp. Overall distance traveled to this point is not quite nine miles.

After dark, Luke recalls that I had told him that the bugs in this area had been almost nonexistent. Perhaps a true statement during the daylight, but it's definitely not the case when traveling down the river at night with a light bulb stuck on your forehead. After swallowing three moths, Luke determines it is better to paddle with his mouth closed, and use the headlamp only when necessary.

A quick look at the GPS and Luke calculates that Silver Maple Campsite, the chosen destination for this evening is roughly three miles ahead. Minutes later, Luke comes across the same downed trees his "cherished friends" had struggled with a few days before. The only difference is they traveled during the day and with much lighter, almost empty boats. Dead falls between this point and Silver Maple Campsite force Luke out of his boat a total of eight times – eight times of either standing on a mucky river bottom and pushing his boat over trees, or crawling up on shore and dragging his boat around the obstacles. Luke's progress slows greatly, and to make a bad situation worse, the moon is hidden by the dense cloud cover. It is casket-dark and rain is beginning to fall.

Luke's mind games are no longer focused on making good time, but instead on movies like the *Blair Witch Project, Deliverance, and Friday the 13th Part III*. Then, while replaying the scariest of the scary scenes, the beaver (not the brother to Wally Cleaver, but the cousin to the extinct giant beaver [Castoroides ohioensis] that terrorized Minnesota wetlands 12,000 years ago) enters stage-right perceiving Luke as a threat to their tranquility. Several times, as Luke is almost upon these intriguing little animals and more unaware of their presence than they are of his, the beaver sound the alarm of an intruder with a piercing crack of their big flat tail crashing down on top the water. It's a sound that in the calm of pitch-black darkness will take its toll on the steadiest of nerves.

One such encounter occurs at a time when there is no way around a deadfall. The shore on river-left is long grass and underbrush with a sharp three foot drop to the water. Luke checks the depth of the river next to the bank. It's at least four feet to the soft bottom. In the darkness, Luke assumes the far side of the river is no better. He is standing upright in his kayak with one hand gripping a clump of brush on shore and the other hand on his paddle suspended in midair for balance about to make his move to dry land when suddenly, "BAM!" a beaver slaps the water within an arm's reach away. With heart pounding and his entire body trembling, Luke responds with his own battle cry of not so carefully chosen words clearly reserved for precisely such a moment as this. Somehow Luke manages to keep his balance though and makes a successful exit.

"What is madness but nobility of soul at odds with circumstance?" -Theodore Roethke, poet (1908–1963)

Almost immediately after getting back into his boat on the downstream side of the last portage, a tough decision must be made. Another strainer is blocking the river. It looks like there is scarcely enough space between it and the water, but he may be able to squeeze under. Luke questions his own judgment as he scrunches down inside the cockpit while leaning way back and inches forward slipping under the tree. It turns out to be a bad call. He is now pinned under the tree with his face squished against the rear deck of the boat. He can do nothing but laugh; not a "ha ha funny" laugh, but more like an "I am not going to make it through this," desperation type laugh.

More scrunching and wriggling and at last Luke escapes the squeeze with a few minor scratches.

That's it. The clogged river is now behind him and there are no more fallen trees. It has taken slightly more than an hour to travel the last two and a half miles. Rules are rules. No PowerAde break is allowed.

Focused again on making miles, Luke reaches US Highway 2 realizing he has paddled past the campsite where he was planning to spend the night. He pulls out the map to locate the next campsite. It is near Stump Lake, nine miles down river. From his current position, Luke believes the campsite on Stump Lake is in the vicinity of where frequent lightning strikes have been occurring for the past half-hour. Determined to press on, he casts logic to the wind and begins paddling.

Waves break over the bow as the paddle across Lake Irving begins as does the rain, but the rain is a mere discomfort. Being out on open water with lightning is a much greater concern. The mile-wide Lake Irving is put to the rear in less than fifteen minutes in spite of the increasing headwind.

Paddling the channel between Lake Irving and Lake Bemidji, Luke ponders the different motel options within walking distance; however, he is not sure if he wants to deal with any dim-witted questions along the way, or how he would fit his kayak in a motel room.

Somewhat hesitant to go on across Lake Bemidji without an update on the storm, a call home to wife, Traci, is made. She agrees to check the radar on the computer and he agrees to wait twenty minutes and call back. Only a few minutes pass before Luke runs low on patience and he decides the wait is not worth it. He starts out, keeping close to the south shoreline instead of cutting straight across. The detour through the thick bulrushes and presumably safer waters adds an extra mile of paddling to the otherwise two mile stretch of open water. It's midnight when Luke locates the river channel on the east shore. He makes the call home for the updated weather report. Good news. The storm appears to be turning to the north. Other than the wind, there shouldn't be any major concerns. He wishes Traci a good night, and continues the journey even though exhaustion is beginning to set in. The campsite on Stump Lake should be four miles up ahead.

Four raccoons are staring at Luke from the shore where the map says the campsite is located – raccoons but no campsite. Luke tells the raccoons to go eat garbage then starts looking for any open clearing that will suffice for the night. A grassy spot down the shore looks to be as good as any. Luke has paddled over six hours and twenty-two miles since starting the trip. He tosses his sleeping bag inside the tent and crawls in on top of it without changing from his wet clothes – too late and too tired.

"We must learn to regard people less in the light of what they do or omit to do, and more in the light of what they suffer."
-Dietrich Bonhoeffer, theologian and writer (1906–1945)

Friday, August 19, 2005

Luke awakens not too much past seven still groggy from not only last evening's workout, but also the week of traveling. Pulling back the tent flap, he is glad to see the storm has passed and the sun is shining. He is not so glad to see a sign no more than ten yards to the left of his abode: "THIS PROPERTY PATROLLED BY NORTHERN SECURITY". Closer than that, to the right, is a pathway through the narrow hedge leading to a house with two cars parked in the drive. No campfire. No breakfast. Just get on the river and get out of here.

Muscle strain and the low level of energy are not easily ignored. Thoughts of giving in and quitting are frequent, but suppressed. Instead, a slower pace is set for the first segment of today's trip. It takes forty-five minutes to get to Ottertail Power Co. Dam, only two miles from his campsite.

Luke makes the two hundred yard portage and then begins paddling below the dam. It is literally 'a real drag' due to low water. It is worse for him than when we paddled this stretch last week. His boat is sitting a lot lower because: (a) 40 lbs of gear we didn't have and (b) 40 lbs of extra body weight we don't have.

Even in the protection of the river channel and the thick forest of hardwoods, Luke is very aware of the east wind ramping up as the sun rises above the horizon. Life has definitely been better. Venting his foul mood, he makes a voodoo doll out of weeds found floating on the river and smashes it with his paddle. The doll represents people he refuses to name, but they know who they are!!!

Giving no thought to what lies ahead, Luke presses on at a steady rate and does not take time for any kind of true rest. The morning simply unrolls in a blur as fatigue runs unbridled.

The last stretch is across Cass Lake where waves are being assembled on the east side well over seven unobstructed miles away, and set into motion like robotic soldiers marching off to war. The three foot waves hit the kayak head on, tossing bucket after bucket of water into Luke's face with the timing of a metronome. Each stroke of the paddle is a battle onto itself, but there is no other option than to continue the fight straight forward into the face of the enemy as it unleashes one battalion after another.

Arriving at the final destination, Knutson Dam, at two in the afternoon, Luke expels the last of his energy as he takes four hard strokes sending the bow of the kayak up on the sand beach next to the boat landing. He lets out a deep breath and throws his paddle out ahead. It falls and bounces once, landing on the shore ten feet or so from two folks who are preparing to go out fishing. Luke slowly lifts himself from the cockpit and exits his boat, collapsing face-up on dry land. The soon-to-be fishermen look over and without concern ask Luke where he started. He no sooner begins to tell the story and they respond, "Well, at least you had nice weather."

Luke continues with his tale about numerous trees blocking the river, swarms of annoying insects, the exasperating experience with the beaver, lightning, tornado warnings, and the unrelenting wind in his face the whole time. The fishermen either choose to ignore him or perhaps have difficulty understanding the incoherent murmurings. Without any further acknowledgment, they push off, leaving Luke lying on shore wishing he would have at least gotten their names so he could add them to his list of "cherished friends."

"Do not be too quick to assume your enemy is a savage just because he is your enemy. Perhaps he is your enemy because he thinks you are a savage. Or perhaps he is afraid of you because he feels that you are afraid of him. And perhaps if he believed you are capable of loving him he would no longer be your enemy." -Thomas Merton, writer (1915–1968)

[Leg 3]

Knutson Dam to Jacobson, MN;
115.5 River Miles

Friday, September 16, 2005

Andy and I arrive at the Knutson Dam Campground early in the evening. It is closed for the season and there is no supply of firewood. We set up camp outside the gate in a picnic area, near the boat landing on the west side of the campground entrance.

I go off to see what I can scrounge up for firewood. When I return half-carrying, half-dragging a large armload of dry timber, I see blood trickling from my thumb. Lesson learned... check all firewood for barbed wire, especially if the firewood bears a remarkable resemblance to fence posts. I discover two more puncture wounds; one in each forearm. Andy says he hopes that my tetanus shot is current. He reminds me of one of the very few by-laws of the Itasca Kayakers, "No one should ever be left behind, UNLESS stricken with lockjaw."

Not certain about the shot, and not going to worry about it, I reach for my *Deluxe First Aid Kit*. There is no doubt in my mind that the antiseptic ointment will protect against any possible infection. "This stuff can cure everything but the common cold and a broken heart."

First things first though, there is an incredible sunset begging to be captured on film. (FYI – As predicted, my wounds do heal over the next two days without becoming infected. No cliff-hanger here.)

In the fast disappearing daylight, I gather more firewood and reduce it into useable lengths while Andy erects the tents. He begins with his tent first. It goes up quickly. Of course, why wouldn't it? It's a youth size pup tent. It is Andy's emergency just-in-case-you-need-a-tent tent which he carries in the trunk of his car, along with a vast variety of other just-in-case crap. He explains that he did not bring his hammock due to the rain in the forecast and his good tent is on his sailboat up on Rainy Lake. He's proud to point out that the tent was purchased a couple years ago at Wal-Mart for only twenty bucks, and that he can actually fit inside; diagonally.

"Wow! Who knows how much it would have cost at say, ah… Toys-R-Us?"

Brian, Tony and Tony's brother Jim who lives in the Twin Cities, arrive well after dark. Andy and I welcome their addition to the conversation, not to mention the cold beverages that they were thoughtful enough to bring. Another hour passes before Luke arrives. Getting out of his truck, he spots Andy's tent and is surprised, "Hey! Thanks to whoever brought the tent for my shoes."

Ready to settle down in the cool fall night, the sight of lightning on the western horizon calls for a check for the current forecast. Andy tunes in his marine radio to Mr. Monotone, the most famous weatherman of all. "Expect a storm with trouble maker winds."

"How dreadful knowledge of the truth can be when there's no help in the truth." -Sophocles, (495–405 BCE)

Saturday, September 17, 2005

An hour before dawn, thunder and lightning announce the approaching storm with much more gusto than Mr. Monotone had hours earlier. The trouble maker winds take down two side poles of Tony's tent, causing it to cave inward. Somehow it remains erect. The storm is enough to cause Brian to evacuate his hammock and move to his car. Everyone else stays where they are.

The wind and rain stop, and clouds dissipate at sunrise. I am still awake so I get up and go out to rekindle the fire. Next, Brian gets out of his GM tent and the others appear shortly after. When discussing the wind and lightning, Andy maintains that he wasn't even aware there was a storm. He "slept like a baby." Guess that's because he had to lie in a fetal position all night in order to fit in his tent.

If we don't spend time cooking, maybe we'll get an earlier start on the paddling thing. Breakfast is bananas, apples, cold cereal, hot oatmeal, breakfast bars, and fruit juice. At 8:30, we're in good shape. Boats and gear are water-ready, sitting at the landing. All that is left to do is to pack up the campsite and move a car to the take-out. Tonight's take-out and campsite are one and the same; Plug Hat Point on the east side of Lake Winnibigoshish.

Somehow, in less than five minutes, we go from thinking *we're almost ready to get on the river,* to, "Let's play golf!" Tony has his clubs and a couple of Nerf golf balls in his car. The game of trying to hit various objects with a phony ball soon escalates to using a real ball and more difficult targets. After an hour of golfing and goofing, Andy and I leave to drop a car. Another hour passes before returning from our mission. It's not until

11:00 that we begin paddling. Our hope is to log in at least eighty miles in the next three days.

"Our heads are round so that thoughts can change direction." -Francis Picabia, painter and poet (1879–1953)

One mile downstream, we paddle under MN State Highway 39. A note on the MN DNR map states, "This is a gentle stretch of river, bordered by mixed hardwood forest. Most of the land is publicly owned; paddlers will see little development past this point. The river leaves the Mississippi Headwaters Board's 'Scenic' designation and enters a section managed as 'Wild.'" How much more wild could it be? A small northern pike surprises Tony. The fish shoots out of the water just ahead of his paddle on the right and jumps over the top of his kayak to the other side. His brother, Jim, sees this and reaches for his fishing rod. Andy suggests that he simply suspend a Dare Devil above the water. Neither dragging a line below nor dangling above yields a catch.

"The unconscious mind is decidedly simple, unaffected, straight-forward and honest. It hasn't got all of this facade, this veneer of what we call adult culture. It's rather simple, rather childish. It is direct and free." -Milton H. Erikson, psychiatrist (1901–1980)

Nine miles from today's start and still a mile west of the big lake, the major topic of discussion is the wind. Again, referencing the MN DNR river map… "Lake Winnibigoshish means dirty water in the language of the Ojibwe, referring to the effect of the wind on the lake's sandy shoreline. Lake Winnibigoshish, or Big Winnie, is Minnesota's third largest lake. A slight breeze can produce large waves across it. **Caution**: *Do not paddle {fourteen miles} across Lake Winnibigoshish. Portage from Reese Landing by car to the Winnie Dam Recreation Area on the east side of the lake. If you must paddle, do so only in warm weather and stay within swimming distance of the shore."* (According to accounts written by other Mississippi River paddlers, they generally take the DNR's advice, adding an extra day to the trip.)

Andy checks with Mr. Monotone and finds out that a front is coming in. The now present 15–20 mph wind from the southeast is expected to shift around to the southwest over the next two hours. This means we may luck out and have the wind pushing on our back side across the big body of water. Our strategy is to paddle to Reese's Landing located on the west shore where the river enters the lake. There we'll have lunch, giving more time for the front to change the wind's direction.

Reese's Landing is not easily located and when found, it is not a desirable picnic site. The cabin next door has a dock. No one is home to grant permission so the assumption is made that the landowner would be happy to share the dock with absolutely anyone. Over lunch, I recall that a co-worker had mentioned he may be fishing on Winnie today. I give him a call on his cell phone to get a first-hand weather report. "Strong winds with waves over three feet. And, if you're interested, fishing isn't any good."

Discussion is brief before we vote. It's unanimous – go straight across the fourteen miles. No portaging and no following the shoreline. Luke, Tony, and Brian will paddle out ahead. Andy, Jim S., and I are to bring up the rear. The first mile or so is a little choppy and not bad at all; however, when we reach the real open water, it is painfully obvious that the wind has shifted only slightly to the southwest. Waves over the three foot mark are coming directly at our small crafts from the right (that'd be starboard to you sailors). For the next seven miles or so, the waves remain unchanged for the most part, though some four-plus foot rollers appear intermittently to make life more interesting. Even with a distance of less than ten yards between the boats, they drop completely out of sight from one another, then reappear atop the next crest. Going slow and cautious gives me time to pray longer prayers and by the grace of God we make it across safely, thirty minutes after the sun sets.

At the landing, we again find the campground closed and again, the tents are set up in the picnic area adjacent to the boat landing. I guess we should have been paying closer attention this morning when the car was dropped off. Really, would it have made a difference?

Brian and Luke make a run back to the put-in to pick up the other vehicles. Then it's dinner at a local sports bar called the Gosh Dam Place, where people don't even try to pretend they are in a fine dining establishment.

Sunday, September 18, 2005

In the pre-dawn, before anyone else is awake, Brian sneaks off for home to keep a promise to his nephew.

Breakfast this morning is a repeat of yesterday, except that Andy introduces Spam to the menu. The first attempt to cook the unknown substance on a stick over the fire is a complete disappointment. One side was subjected to more heat than the other, and the whole thing came out burned beyond recognition. The container is checked for preparation instructions and nowhere does it state, "Mount on a stick. Burn real good over an open fire. Then discard." Another shot at cooking the remaining portion of the delicacy proves to be successful and receives great reviews.

"All wholesome food is caught without a net or trap."
-William Blake, poet, engraver, and painter (1757–1827)

More golf is played by some while others pack up the camp. Afterward, the car shuffle takes place. Tony and his brother, Jim, have to leave for home tonight, so my SUV and the trailer along with Tony's car are parked at Schoolcraft State Park. The take-out is thirty-one river miles downstream. Since neither vehicle has the required park pass nor is there an attendant on duty when we arrive, the vehicles are abandoned directly in front of the office. That way if or when a ranger does show up for work, it will be easier for him to issue a ticket.

Once more, it's 11:00 before we are on the water. If nothing else, we have proven to be consistent. After a few minutes of paddling, we enter Little Winnibigoshish. Four white pelicans and a small flock of mallard ducks at the mouth of the river are caught off guard and take flight. There is not much conversation as we cross the lake and enter the river channel on the other side. Then Andy makes it known that he has calculated that it requires an average of four hundred twenty-five paddle strokes to move his boat downstream one-half mile in a current that is slightly less than 2 mph. He asks each of the paddlers how much they would have to be paid if they were to sit in an all white room, in a line, and pull twenty-five thousand times with each hand on a rope that poses a varying resistance of three to ten pounds – the equivalent of paddling thirty miles.

"Can we talk?"

"Yes."

"Can we trade positions in the line?"

"Yes."

"Will there be fresh air?"

"Yes."

"Will someone be there to occasionally spray us in the face with a garden hose?"

"Yes."

"Will there be a change of scenery?"

"No."

The response to the "How much would you have to be paid?" question ranges from $300 to $500.

Then the big question, "How is pulling on a rope in an all white room different than what we're doing?"

"We're not in an all white room. We're out in the midst of God's creation with the element of surprise around each and every bend, making the experience on the river priceless."

"The truth is that our finest moments are most likely to occur when we are feeling deeply uncomfortable, unhappy, or unfulfilled. For it is only in such moments, propelled by our discomfort, that we are likely to step out of our ruts and start searching for different ways or truer answers." -**M. Scott Peck, psychiatrist and author (1936–2005)**

It's worthy to note that there is no "Ben Stinks" painted on the underside of the US Hwy 2 Bridge. Either Ben has cleaned up his act or his "cherished friends" have run out of paint.

Lunch is at Gambler's Point, a campsite set on top of a thirty foot ridge covered with beautiful full-grown white pines overlooking the river below. According to the MN DNR, "This is the only access to land from the river as it makes its way through a series of oxbows, created as the river cut channels in soft material laid down by glaciers. Many of these had been dredged during logging years to provide a more direct route for log movement."

(View from Gambler's Point)

With twelve miles to go, before reaching Schoolcraft Park, we decide that it would be best to stick closer together. The map shows the river as a maze with at least ten tributaries and oxbows on the upstream side of White Oak Lake. All the tributaries bear the same name: Mississippi River. During the spring run off when the water is high, navigation through this area can be quite difficult because there are so many opportunities to get turned around. That is not the case today, however, and for the first time since the beginning of this journey at the Headwaters, we are feeling good about having set out so late in the season. The smaller tributaries and oxbows are close to being dry, making the main channel easy to find.

Both daylight and energy levels are dwindling at a rapid rate. It is difficult to say which is in the lead as we close in on the last three miles before the take-out. It's Luke, who suggests singing, and before long we are reenergized. The singing does nothing about the sun. Some folks working in their backyards along the river (the first people we've seen all day) enjoy the tunes and provide positive feedback.

"He who sings scares away his woes." -**Miguel de Cervantes, novelist (1547–1616)**

It is dark when we reach Schoolcraft Campground after nine hours of paddling the winding river. Even though the campground is open for business, there won't be any camping tonight. It took very little discussion earlier today to make this decision. The choice was between hot showers, a hot home-cooked meal, cold beer, and soft beds at my house in Grand Rapids ten miles away, or none of the above here at the state operated Schoolcraft Park.

Monday, September 19, 2005

Rain is falling but the forecast is for clearing skies. If we lolly-gag long enough, maybe the rain will pass. We do and it does.

Luke, Andy, and I are on water at 10:30. We paddle steadily, but with little conversation as we embrace the solitude, soaking in the beauty of the fall morning that surrounds us. The clouds give way to a blue sky and a brilliant sun that rejuvenates the wildlife in the wake of the rain. Over a dozen herons are seen wading in the shallows. Two otters playing and chasing each other on the river bank pay no attention to the kayaks as we pass by. Time and time again, the bays of wild rice come alive with a thunderous roar as huge flocks of migrating waterfowl take to the air, only to land again a few hundred yards away.

After a total of seventeen miles, we exit the river on the upstream side of the Blandin Paper Company Dam in Grand Rapids. Andy's car was left here on Friday and mine was dropped off this morning. Andy heads for home and I give Luke a ride back to Schoolcraft as part of the car shuffle. It is labeled as another good day.

Tuesday, September 20, 2005

The rugged landscape and many lakes in the region around Grand Rapids are a direct result of the last ice age (extending beyond the annual, nine-month-long event that comes without mercy or hesitation). About 13,000 years ago, a warming trend in the earth's atmosphere began to melt the glaciers. Vast amounts of glacial melt-water flowed across the land, forming a network of streams and rivers. Basins carved by the glaciers filled with melting ice to form lakes (over 10,000 in Minnesota with 1,000 of them here in Itasca County). Twelve thousand years ago, the glaciers retreated from Minnesota. The warming climate allowed Mega-fauna such as wooly mammoths, mastodon, and giant ground sloths (presumably ancestors of the beaver) to move into Northern Minnesota. [2]

Being close to home has its benefits. Short paddling outings in the evenings and on weekends are quite doable without having to take time off from work or do any camping, much less be concerned about complicated logistics. As Andy and I head out this afternoon, it is without Luke due to work and without Tony due to school – more makeup sessions. Two other club members, Craig Holgate, a local radio announcer, and Ana Jasso, my niece, join us at the put-in at Steamboat Access in downtown Grand Rapids.

An unprompted game of 'bumper boats' begins no more than a hundred yards from getting underway. There are no rules of engagement to the game. It usually starts with one or more paddlers sneaking up on another boat from behind and redirecting the route of the unsuspecting boat into the shoreline, a rock, or some other obstacle by pushing the stern of the forward boat with bow of the attack boat. The game is over after those involved either tire of the battle or have gotten sufficiently wet from the accompanying paddle splashing and one surrenders.

"War, at first, is the hope that one will be better off; next, the expectation that the other fellow will be worse off; then, the satisfaction that he isn't any better off; and, finally, the surprise at everyone's being worse off." - **Karl Kraus, writer (1874–1936)**

The trip on this outstanding fall afternoon under clear skies is the eight mile stretch from Steamboat Access below the Blandin Dam to the Itasca County 441 Access. It takes a little over two hours. Afterward, gear is loaded up and then it's off to my house for bonfire and picnic.

Monday, October 10, 2005

It's Columbus Day, an office holiday for Blandin employees and a perfect day to set sail. The temperature is a balmy 28 F, with

"Ka-Ka-Ska-Ska"

a promised high of 60+F accompanied with blue skies. Luke and I meet for breakfast at the Silver Spoon Café in Grand Rapids. Andy is not along today because of a last minute decision to go to Philadelphia (the city not the state) to see his sister who is there on a short visit from London. Andy admits that it would be good to see his sister but the real purpose of the trip is to see his new three month old nephew, Luca.

"Call it a clan, call it a network, call it a tribe, call it a family: Whatever you call it, whoever you are, you need one."
-Unknown

(Morning mist)

Fog rises from the river as the sun positions itself above the tree line. Luke and I enter the water from Itasca County 441

Access (part of a make up session for Luke). Today's plan is to paddle to the Jacobson Campground, where my wife, Sharron, will provide a ride back to the put-in.

We can't help but notice along the river how many of the aspen, a foot or more in diameter, have fallen victim to the local beaver. Less than three inches at the center of each tree is all that remains to support the mass above – okay, they haven't 'fallen' yet. Dozens of these *Populus tremuloides,* now devoid of their normally trembling leaves, are nothing more than tall skeletons showing off their sense of balance like children in the play yard standing on one foot.

Not long after Luke's harrowing experience with beaver scaring the bejeebies out of him, while paddling alone at night near the Headwaters I decided to gain more knowledge of the beaver. When searching the internet, I found one authority claiming that beaver actually enjoy practical jokes within their community. It is not clear what kind of practical jokes they play or how the person doing the research made such a discovery. But one thing is clear, if you want to learn more about beaver on the internet, you should enter 'beaver animal' and not just simply 'beaver'.

"If I had six hours to chop down a tree, I'd spend the first hour sharpening the axe". -Abraham Lincoln, 16th President of the U.S. (1809–1865)—*"If I had six hours to cut down a tree, I'd get a chain saw and do it in ten minutes."* -Greg Hagy, millwright (1957-)

A short break is taken to lighten the burden of morning coffee and to share a candy bar. Both Luke and I have recently read the book, *One Good Story*, by Ron Severs, an interesting tale of the author's forty-four days paddling the Mississippi from the Headwaters to New Orleans in a kayak borrowed from his neighbor. It is Luke who points out that nowhere in the one hundred forty-eight pages of the book does Author Ron mention having gone to the bathroom. Not even a hint on the subject! However, he did write of sleeping in an outhouse one night along the trail rather than putting up his tent in inclement weather. So did Ron consciously decide to omit discussion regarding human waste in his book, or does this explain how he managed to paddle an average of fifty miles per day?

"Persons appear to us according to the light we throw upon them from our own minds." -Laura Ingalls Wilder, author (1867–1957)

Luke and I have covered twenty miles and it's time for lunch. There on the east side of the river, on top of a vertical twelve foot high bank, is the MN DNR designated canoe campsite – probably more accessible by land than by water. The west side of the river is much more approachable. Instead of sitting at the MN DNR picnic table, we find a fallen tree that suits our bottoms quite comfortably.

Luke is surprised that eating is part of today's plan, even though it was spelled out in detail in an email sent to him late last week: "Bring a sandwich, beverage, and a snack to share." Ironically, Luke had stopped at a convenience store while in route this morning to get some PowerAde. He says he thought briefly about getting food stuff, but then dismissed the idea. *"We're paddling just thirty miles. We shouldn't have to stop for lunch or anything like that."* PowerAde was on sale though: two bottles for $2.22 plus tax. At the counter, the lady said, "The total is $2.36." Luke had exactly 36 cents in his pocket to put with his two ones.

Both Luke and Clerk Lady commented, "What are the odds?!"

Luke does some quick math and works out the probability... "Oh yeah, one in a hundred – truly astonishing (in a sarcastic tone)."

Clerk Lady, "Uh?"

Luke is the math wizard of the group. Back in July of this year, the club was paddling an eleven mile section of the Swan River in Northern Minnesota. Craig Holgate brought along his thirty-something sister, LeeAnn, who had not paddled very much prior to the trip. Craig assured her it would be okay. "It's just an afternoon float trip downstream."

That section of the Swan, however, was no different than the previous forty miles of the Swan (that Craig had not paddled) narrow, crooked, and more times than not, restricted with trees that stretched from one bank to the other. Navigation was difficult at best.

The Itasca Kayakers entered the Swan that afternoon at 4:30 and within the first two hours, LeeAnn had already experienced two wet exits (wet' ek'sit, wet' eg'zit; intransitive verb – to fall out of your kayak for no apparent reason), climbed over or portaged around windfalls and strainers too numerous to count, lost one of her sandals and a toe ring, waded through mud and muck up to her hips, and was being eaten alive by blood thirsty mosquitoes and insensitive deer flies. No need to mention she wasn't having a great deal of fun. Then during a brief break, someone asked the time. "It's 6:30. We're averaging 1.5 mph. There are eight more miles to go, and the sun will be setting in less than three hours."

Luke put his head down on the deck of his boat and sighed, "I wish I hadn't paid such close attention to second grade math! At this rate we won't get off the river until midnight."

"Ka-Ka-Ska-Ska"

"All kids are gifted; some just open their packages earlier than others." -Michael Carr, composer (1905–1968)

Fortunately on that day, the Swan River soon straightened out, got wider and had fewer obstacles. We made it to the take-out shortly after the sun set. Unfortunately, LeeAnn has not been seen on another club outing since. I received a photo via email from Craig the following day of LeeAnn's arms looking like a classic case of small pox.

"To suffering there is a limit; to fearing, none." -Francis Bacon, essayist, philosopher, and statesman (1561–1626)

The above event has absolutely nothing to do with the trip down the Mississippi, but if this journal ever gets published into a book, the more people mentioned, the more potential buyers created. Too bad Luke wasn't thinking of that this morning at the convenience store, he could have asked for the name of Clerk Lady.

Back to today....Lunch time, in case you forgot. I offer to share my peanut butter and pickle sandwich with Luke.

Luke declines. He says he does not particularly care for pickles. He goes on, "As a matter of fact, if it was tomorrow, and we had been paddling since this morning and I was offered the same incredible entrée, I would still reply with an emphatic 'No!'. Furthermore, if it was the day after tomorrow, and we had been paddling for two days without having eaten anything, I would then be inclined to at least hesitate before refusing the offer." Luke does, however, accept the extra pudding snack, a chocolate bar, and a package of cheese and crackers that I have in my bag.

When done with lunch, we return to the mission and arrive at the Jacobson Campground at 3:20 after thirty miles of paddling today.

Friday, October 14, 2005

Andy, Ana, and I meet at Herb Beer's Access off County Road 3 about ten miles south of Grand Rapids along with Tony and another new face, Tom Frick. Tom lives in Grand Rapids, is married and the father of two teenage girls. Tom enjoys doing things other people simply talk about. Each year, he and a group of friends go on a high adventure vacation such as paddling the Quetico, Yellowstone National Park, or Lake Superior around Isle Royal: biking the Bad Lands of South Dakota; or the ultra-light backpacking trip two years ago through Superior National Forest.

"Time is the least thing we have of." -Ernest Hemingway, author (1899–1961)

The group is once again repeating a portion of the river to allow Andy and Tony a chance to make up for not being available on the last trip. To save time this afternoon, Andy and I have already dropped Andy's car and trailer off at the take-out at the Jacobson Campground.

Things are pretty quiet the first two hours as everyone seems to be enjoying the blue sky, warm temperatures, and the 15–20 mph wind, but only when it is at our backside.

Around the half-way point of our trip, three eagles are perched in the trees forty yards up ahead. The mom eagle and one of the youngsters take flight and settle in the trees farther back on the opposite shore. The other youngster stays behind, reluctant to respond to us as we pass directly beneath it sitting on a limb not more than fifteen feet above the river.

It's about this time that Tom offers up Guinness Draught he has stashed somewhere within his boat. Everyone except Ana accepts. Tom is complimented on his taste in barley brew and humbly responds, "It was a choice between this and Hamms. Though both are very similar, I chose Guinness because of the size of the can."

Not to be outdone, Tony passes around a jar of dry roasted nuts, and soon after, some Honeyberry Backwoods cigars. Ana declines the option of a cigar too. Life is good. It's a magic time of day with the sun sinking fast creating an awkward silence along the river. The song birds begin their silent retreat giving way to their nocturnal buddies.

We have paddled slightly more than seventeen miles since the put-in, and have six miles to go. The sun has been replaced with an amazing harvest moon rising above the tree tops, casting shadows of the forest across the water all around us. Tony starts to sing an Irish drinking song but Andy puts a check on it as he takes out his harmonica, and does a great job on *Amazing Grace*.

Over the past three years, the club has done their fair share of paddling after sundown, and yet each time there is a sense of new found adventure. We continue on in the darkness, occasionally coming close to half-submerged trees easily hidden in their own camouflage. A couple of beaver show frustration with the infringement on their turf with a slap of the tail. And off in the forest, the mystifying thud of a toppling tree momentarily silences the barred owl. There is no doubt about it – being on the water after dark puts you in touch with nature at an entirely different dimension than during the day.

"Nature is ever at work building and pulling down, creating and destroying, keeping everything whirling and flowing, allowing no rest but in rhythmical motion, chasing

everything in endless song out of one beautiful form into another." -John Muir, Naturalist and explorer (1838–1914)

(Shift change)

As we come around the last bend in the river before our take-out, the flickering of campers' lanterns at the campground next to the landing make it impossible for us to miss our stop.

Trip Report
- 205.0 miles completed (8.9% of total trip)
- 2,102.0 to The Gulf

[Leg 4]
Jacobson, MN to Aitkin, MN;
84.0 River Miles

Saturday, November 5, 2005

Today is the opening of white-tail deer season in Minnesota. Approximately 500,000 men, women and children dressed head to toe in blaze orange will be traipsing through the wilderness toting large caliber hunting rifles, complemented with telescopic sights bearing the same quality of optics found in the Hubble Space Telescope, all hoping to tangle with an elusive trophy buck and come out the winner. Andy says, "The sport of deer hunting comes down to a case of either us (humans) or them (deer). You can tell by the look in a deer's eyes as it stares you down from the edge of the highway that it's a good thing the tables are not turned. The only thing saving us is the fact we invented the gun before they could."

The plan is to be "on the water" at the Jacobson Campground no later than 7:15. There are thirty-five miles of river between here and Big Sandy Lake and less than ten hours of daylight.

Andy, Luke, Joan, and I are at the landing as the day breaks from a soggy overnight low of 36 F. To save time, I abandon the other three to do the unloading so I can look for Tony and Brian who had said they were going to stay here at the campground last night. They did this to avoid the hassles of packing and driving the fifty miles over from Chisholm early this morning. Getting up early defies practically all of Tony's sleeponomics' principles.

Only five minutes elapse before I report back that Brian and Tony cannot be found in the campground. Andy calls their cell phones. No answer. The worst is assumed; they were on their way here last night, got caught in some sort of time warp and are currently suspended in cosmos well above the Manicouagan Reservoir in northern Quebec.

Time's wasting, and while we are in the process of deciding what to do, Brian and Tony drive up to the landing. Not trapped in a time warp at all, they've been up since 6:00 and thought the meeting time wasn't until 7:30. The two had been camping on the far end of the camp ground, way beyond where I stopped looking. Conclusion: I suck at reconnaissance.

Minnesota law requires hunters and trappers to wear blaze orange on their upper body while in the woods during deer season. The law does not apply to anyone on the water. However, wearing blaze orange in a war zone where the code of the land is "If it's brown – it's down" makes real good sense whether you're a hunter or not. With that in mind, I purchased a two-dollar stocking cap and a five-dollar nylon mesh vest of the appropriate color for this weekend's trip. As I slip the vest on over my PFD, my comrades erupt in a howl of laughter. (It is clear they are quite envious of my fine attire.) Luke, being the most envious of all, finally gains some self-control, "I think your blaze orange open-mesh vest, with a daring mix of 'delicate and racy' is rather stunning. However, it is probably better suited for a super model in Victoria's Secret's Outdoor Life Collection than on an old guy set to conquer the Mighty Mississippi."

"Civilization is the encouragement of differences."
-Mohandas Karamchand Gandhi (1869–1948)

"Ka-Ka-Ska-Ska"

Three miles downstream from the put-in, two fellows wearing jeans, flannel shirts and blaze orange hats are seen standing near river's edge at the wayside rest in Jacobson. Judging by the look of relief on their faces, it is surmised that they have just finished using the historical Ron Severs Cabin. The "Cabin" is the actual outhouse where Ron slept while on his adventure down the Mississippi.

Earlier, it was determined that Andy would be in charge of counting the number of hunters seen along the way. "Don't forget to count those two at the wayside rest as the first ones."

"No. They looked more like gatherers."

Andy's decision is questioned, taking into account the blaze orange hats, "We are also wearing blaze orange and not hunters. And, consider the fact that Jim is not hunting nor performing a burlesque act in his dainty little blaze orange vest. How would we count him?" The decision stands.

"The only wisdom we can hope to acquire is the wisdom of humility: Humility is endless." -T.S Eliot, poet (1888–1965)

Lunch is at Ms. Keto Campsite (No, really, that's the name of the place.) Joan does not disappoint us. She has brought fresh produce from her garden to dress up the otherwise plain sandwiches. No one has anything to cook but you can't let perfectly good firewood go to rot. Brian lights a fire, but because things are still quite damp from yesterday's rain, it takes a while to get it going. Andy, the Eagle Scout, offers to help and when he moves only one of the sticks slightly, the fire takes off with a low roar. He says, "It's the volume knob."

"How is it one careless match can start a forest fire, but it takes a whole box to start a campfire?" -Unkown

Break is over and it's back to the trip. Once we are all settled into the boats, Luke proclaims, "It's game time! We're going to play 20 questions." Or as it turns out on a couple of rounds, 120 questions like when it is my turn to pick a 'place' for others to guess. The assumption is that I will pick a city, country or other geographic location. It's always bad to assume but anyone will tell you it is especially bad when it concerns me. After 100+ questions the location of the secret place is narrowed down to within three inches of the bottom half of my head. Brian finally gets the correct answer – the tip of my nose. At that point, the others realize that I should not be allowed to play games – in addition to not being allowed to do reconnaissance.

The sun sets as scheduled at 5:00, taking away all but a trace of light for the last two miles. Where the Mississippi is joined by the Sandy River, we turn and go upstream a mile in a tough current to get to our campsite. After a total of thirty-five miles today, we arrive at the Sandy Lake Recreation Area. I take charge of building a fire and setting up camp as the others leave in Luke's truck (left here yesterday) to do the car shuffle.

Before lights out, Luke announces he has dibs on any extra gloves I may have brought along, "Just in case someone forgot to bring some."

"Ka-Ka-Ska-Ska"

"My greatest skill has been to want but little." -Henry David Thoreau, naturalist and author (1817–1862)

Sunday, November 6, 2005

Brian prepares a hearty breakfast of eggs and bacon for everyone – except Joan of course. Afterward, Luke, Andy, and Joan get ready to take vehicles to the take-out. Before leaving, I offer Luke maps of the river. Luke gives the maps only a cursory review and leaves them behind since he has another copy in his truck. After getting five miles down the road, he realizes his map set is not complete. He does not have the page showing the take-out location. He presses on. "It can't be that hard to find."

The car shufflers drop two cars off at a river access beside US Highway 169 they believe is the take-out. They are not a hundred percent certain it is the correct take-out but, if wrong, the right one is most likely within a couple of miles anyway.

The kayaks are on the water at 9:30. I am not sure if we are getting more efficient or if the overnight low of 34 F is the motivating factor.

Nine miles downstream Luke notices a common theme pertaining to the many buildings along the river. "Why do you suppose they're all built with rotting wood and patches of shingles that have gone missing?" He also notes that many have been constructed with crooked, swayback roofs, like caricatures of outbuildings in a Norman Rockwell painting. Another observation is the number of lightning rods on the barn roofs. Most have at least five, some have a lot more. Luke envisions how the conversation may have gone between the door-to-door lightning rod salesman and the farmers...

"Ya look like a smart man, but I see ya ain't got no lightnin' rods on top your barn."

"Nope."

"Ain't ya afraid of a fire comin' down out of the sky and levelin' that barn to a pile of ashes?"

"Nope."

"Have ya ever seen a barn hit by lightning?"

"Nope."

"Well, it's like a Model A goin' into a sharp corner and the steering wheel comin' off in yer hands. There ain't nothin' yer gonna do."

"Uh?"

"Yer neighbor, Nester Johnson over in Crow Wing County got lightnin' rods on his new barn. His old barn got hit by lightnin' last year and burned to the ground faster than a cow peein' on a flat rock. But that new barn's got lightnin' rods; kinda like shuttin' the hen house door after the fox carried off the cat. Ya don't want that to happen here do ya?"

"Nope. How many of those lightnin' rods do ya think I need?

"Minimum five. Seven's better. Ten is perfect. Some folks would try to sell ya twelve for a barn that size, but I don't want ya to have to buy somethin' ya don't need."

"I'll take ten."

"Good idea. Ya wouldn't be interested in some Hailentrylithium would ya? Ya put this stuff down on the ground durin' the plantin' of yer seed in the spring and yer crop is 100% guaranteed against hail damage for the first forty-five days of germinaten."

"How much do ya think I'd need for that field o'er there?"

"Oh, let's take a closer look."

"**The function of the imagination is not to make strange things settled, so much as to make settled things strange.**"
-G.K. Chesterton, essayist and novelist (1874–1936)

"Ka-Ka-Ska-Ska"

Lunch is at Berglund County Park in Palisade. The city of Palisade was named by an official of the Soo Railroad Line for the high embankment on either side of the Mississippi River. The city park is a very nice setting overlooking the river with a shelter, picnic tables, and a number of grills to use.

When we get back in the boats, Joan is out ahead of the pack and is focused on only one thing – the finish line twelve miles down river. Between yesterday's paddle and the time on the water so far today, we've covered fifty-four miles. She is thoroughly convinced her limit is closer to twenty-eight miles per week, but she is not about to give in yet.

"To know how to hide one's ability is great skill."
-Francois de LaRochefoucauld, writer (1613–1680)

It's time for another game: 'blind kayaker'. Luke instructs everyone except for Brian to pull their stocking caps down over their faces so they are unable to see where they are going. Brian's job is to guide us as we continue to paddle. We play the game for the next mile.

(Playing blind kayaker)

When we catch up to Joan, we ask if she wants to play too. "No thanks. I think we did that last night on the last couple miles before the campground." We're about to be put in the same situation again. There are forty-five minutes of daylight left and at least ninety minutes of river before getting to the planned take-out north of Aitkin, MN at Hwy 169.

Luke has mentioned several times throughout the day that he thinks the cars are about two miles farther down river than what had been planned, due to the confusion this morning with the maps. I scroll down on my GPS to see if I can find where the cars may have been left. Reluctantly, I inform the others that Hwy 169 does not cross the Mississippi at another location in this area. As I study the map, I realize, however, that Hwy 169 does cross other rivers in the area. "Is it possible our cars are waiting for us on the wrong river?"

Fortunately, Andy had marked the drop-off on his GPS this morning and I had marked the public access on my GPS using a map for reference. Luke calls for a crow-fly report to both points. They are the same. We are confident the cars are at the right landing. Big relief! In Luke's defense, there was no road sign clearly identifying the site this morning.

A few hundred yards past the confluence of the Willow River and the Mississippi, an eight-point buck is struggling to climb the high sand bank. At first it isn't clear if the animal is truly frightened, or if he is trying to escape so as not to be identified as part of a group that would allow one of its members to wear a 'delicate blaze orange lacy' vest. Then it becomes apparent that the buck is wounded. To make matters worse, there are five eagles in the trees not far beyond, waiting for the deer to go to the other end of the food chain.

Two miles downriver, we see a farmer who is outside working in his yard on river-right. Andy gets his attention and tells him of the wounded deer. The farmer says he knows the location and assures us that he and his neighbor will take care of the animal.

Jim Lewis

(Waiting for dinner)

We arrive at the take-out at 8:00, to find the cars patiently waiting in the dark. Tony, Brian, and Joan are leaving after the boats are loaded because of work schedules. Andy, Luke, and I have been planning to take on the next nineteen miles into Aitkin starting tomorrow morning. Due to our high level athletic prowess, however, we've been talking about continuing on tonight. Without any trouble the trip would take almost three hours. After a lot more discussion, and a bit of concern about a set of rapids identified on the MN DNR map, it is finally decided to stick with the original plan. We'll paddle it tomorrow.

There's not really a good place to spend the night here at the landing – not even an outhouse to sleep in, so the intent is to camp in Aitkin and return to this point in the morning. Aitkin is about ten miles away by road.

The temperature is in the mid-30s when we arrive at the campground in Aitkin. It's expected to drop to at least freezing before the night is over. Luke and Andy are going to sleep in their vehicles. I opt to pitch a tent, even though the other two said they would be willing to rent me a car if I wanted one.

Monday, November 7, 2005

We're back at the Waldeck Public Access at 8:30. Soon the boats are in the water, ready for the last nineteen miles of our weekend adventure. Two otters swim out into the river ahead to greet us.

Nine miles from where we started this morning, we stop to gawk at the Aitkin Flood Diversion Channel. Here a fixed dam retains the main channel during low water and allows flood level waters to flow over, spilling into the seven mile long diversion channel. It is the only dam of its type on the entire Mississippi.

The three-day trip is over as we arrive back at the Aitkin Campground where the river steamers Lee, Swan, and Andy Gibson sank. Supposedly the skeleton of the Andy Gibson is visible during low water but either someone's making up the story or we don't know where to look.

By 2:00 pm we're on our way back to Grand Rapids thinking about returning for the next paddle.

Trip Report
- 289.0 miles completed (12.5% of total trip)
- 2,018.0 to The Gulf

[Leg 5]
Aitkin, MN to Brainerd, MN;
53.0 River Miles

Monday, November 21, 2005

Today's forecast is for a high in the mid to upper 30s with a northwest wind at 10–20 mph. Luke, Andy, and I are on the water at 8:45. The distance to the takeout, north of Crosby, is a little over twenty-five miles by river and sixteen miles by road. The river has straightened out for this leg. Upstream the 'winding factor' has been closer to 2.5:1.

Minutes from the landing we see two eagles roosting in the trees above a dead doe on river-right. This is the first of three dead deer found in the next fourteen miles. It may be further evidence that wounded deer tend to run toward water. The other possibility is that this section of river has a number of deer genetically predetermined to be poor swimmers.

Each time the river twists to the northwest, the wind does its best to push the kayaks back upstream with waves breaking over the bows. "Some people think we are crazy for going out in weather like this."

"It is days like this that give credence to their concern."

"Insanity in individuals is something rare - but in groups, parties, nations and epochs, it is the rule." -**Friedrich Nietzsche, philosopher (1844–1900)**

We begin the search for a place to take a lunch break, preferably out of the wind. The search continues for well over two miles. It is not always easy to find a solid shoreline to make a stop. It's usually a choice between either a steep bank right down to river's edge or such a soft shore that your feet (and sometimes your legs) quickly disappear in the muck or, even worse, the shore appears to be solid but in realty it is slipperier than the bathroom floor in a gas station on the Oklahoma Panhandle.

It has been a long thirteen miles without a break and our legs are unsteady as we exit onto a convenient bench of hard beach tucked into the river bank. Years of high water spring run-offs have eroded the stability of the once stately oaks above. Now the trees lean precariously over the river's bank patiently waiting to take their own turn at a float trip down the Mississippi. Behind the trees lay acres of wide open pasture stretching out to the west.

During lunch, a rather large black cow in much need of a bath moseys on down to the river for a drink. Luke lets out a very realistic "moo" which the cow totally ignores. Luke explains that cows don't respond to mooing because they hear it all the time.

I said, if the cow belonged to me, I would name it Rex and then I shout, "Hey Rex!" just to see how it sounds.

The cow nonchalantly lifts his head and peers over at us.

"Wow! What are the chances of guessing a cow's name on the first try?"

The remainder of the trip is similar to the morning with beautiful hardwoods on one side, tall white pines on the other, and water down the center. Though not as cold as it was earlier, the wind is still eager to greet the kayaks around each corner that points northwest.

The only wildlife seen this afternoon is a red fox. Actually Luke is the only one who can lay claim to seeing the perfect chestnut specimen with a distinctive white tip on the end of its bushy tail. Luke stops paddling as soon as he spots the carnivore standing erect and proud on the end of an old dead-grey log that rests inches above the water against a backdrop of blazing fall color on river-right. Luke begins to drift closer, hoping Andy and I would be able to get our cameras out for a great shot. This is not the case. We are completely unaware of the fox even though we are following directly behind Luke. What we do notice though are the corners on Luke's hat. They look exactly like the ears of Mickey Mouse. Luke is now only a few feet from the fox and knows for sure that Ansel Adams and his pal Li'l Ansel are framing and composing the perfect photo, digitally capturing the once in a lifetime event. It's not gonna happen. The Adams twins are still unmindful of the fox and break into song, "M-I-C– –K-E-Y...". The fox, not impressed, turns and trots back to shore disappearing in the tall grass. Luke is even less impressed with the Adams twins.

"If you wish to be loved, show more of your faults than your virtues." -Edward Bulwer-Lytton, author (1803–1873)

Tuesday, November 22, 2005

Luke, Andy, Ana, and I set off on the water at 9:00 from the landing near the bridge where we had taken out yesterday. The temperature is in the mid-twenties and the wind is predicted to be light and variable throughout the day. The river current which has been less than 2 mph for the last hundred miles or so has suddenly gotten faster – at least for a couple hundred yards. Andy sprints ahead, reporting a new record top speed of 9.8 mph!

After ninety minutes of paddling, we enter the confluence of the Pine River, the one-time location of a Native American village where Lieutenant Zebulon Pike stopped on his expedition to the Headwaters in the winter of 1805. Not many years later, an Episcopalian mission was built here. There is no remaining evidence of the mission that can be seen from the river today.

The rest of the morning and early afternoon passes one stroke at a time and is pretty much uneventful. The sign on river-left indicates the Half-Moon Campsite is three hundred yards down stream; possibly a good place for lunch.

The steep bank to access the campsite is only part of the problem at hand. The approach across the bay is a frozen mass, forcing a landing downstream. To get back to the picnic area, it's a fight through underbrush across a small, not-yet-frozen mud bog, and then a climb up a precipitous hill. At the top of the bluff overlooking the river, there is a small clearing suitable to pitch a tent. The State has provided a picnic table and a fire ring. The picnic table is secured with a small 3/16" chain. The fire ring is held to an anchor in the ground with a much larger 1/2" chain. It is deduced that the fire ring is a 'hotter' item on the black market.

Set off to the side of the trail, a few yards away in amongst the leafless undergrowth, is a primitive toilet: a white plastic shroud the size and shape of an upside down five-gallon bucket over a hole in the ground with a plastic seat attached. It's out in the open without the benefit of sidewalls, door, or roof.

No time is taken to build a fire, so lunch is eaten while standing. This is not to say you need a fire to eat sitting down but you do need to stand if you're going to dance and dancing has been a proven method of staying warm since before fire was discovered.

"Ka-Ka-Ska-Ska"

"And those who were seen dancing were thought to be insane by those who could not hear the music." -**Friedrich Wilhelm Nietzsche, philosopher (1844–1900)**

Ana made a comment a few weeks ago, "Real girls don't go to the bathroom in the woods." She now asks the location of the restroom. How could she miss it? It's in plain sight of everything within a thirty foot radius including the picnic table. Ana tells us guys that we must remain facing north until she gives the "all clear." Within moments, we, along with all the little chickadees, and squirrels, and every other creature of the forest within a country mile, are bowled over as little 5'2"Ana lets out an undomesticated screech, "OH MY GOD!! THIS IS COLD!" We intuitively know that this is not the "all clear" but that Ana has become something less than (or greater than) a "real girl."

The commitment to a thirty minute break is forgotten and our stay on dry land is closer to an hour. No sooner are we back on the river when an otter with a head the size of a soccer ball surfaces directly in front of the boats and pauses long enough for the paddlers to get a good look at him but no time for photos.

Four miles from having lunch, Little Rabbit Lake is visible through a narrow ice-covered channel on river-left. Ana and Luke slice their boats through the thinner areas of ice liberating large chunks to float freely down river.

Last year before the club began to go out on icy waters, time was spent reading about hypothermia. Since then, a water-proof dry-bag containing such items as extra clothes, fire starters, chemical hand warmers, and hi-tech space blankets is brought on each trip. While reading up on hypothermia, it was learned that transferring heat to a cold body is best done by removing all clothing and placing a warm body next to the cold one. Even better is to have two warm bodies lie down with the cold person in between. This is referred to as the naked human sandwich. The whole concept of this life-saving technique immediately sparked plenty of discussion within the Itasca Kayakers as to when would be the appropriate time to execute such a plan. Andy hastily volunteered to be the Minister of the Naked Sandwich. He assumed full responsibility to determine not only when to execute the maneuver but also the level of nakedness required for each occurrence. As the Minister he also maintains the right to select the warming participants. There were a couple of people who took a dip in 35–40 degree water last winter and early spring while out paddling; however, they did not experience levels of severe hypothermia indicating the need to deploy the sandwich technique. Meanwhile, Andy continues to wait patiently to wield his power.

An hour before sundown, Andy announces to the group that he is officially tired of this activity (paddling, not waiting to wield his power as Minister of the Naked Sandwich). There is no disagreement. It has been cold all day and there is more wind than anyone cares to deal with at this point. The prediction for "light and variable" was not even close.

"The secret of joy is the mastery of pain." -**Anais Nin, writer (1903–1977)**

With the sun nearing the horizon, we pass through the French Rapids Access, an area of rugged relief where the banks rise a dramatic hundred feet above the river. A man with a rifle at the river's edge, along the hiking trail, is picking something up as we paddle by. We wave but the man does not wave back. Instead, he takes whatever he has retrieved from the river and places it at the base of a tree. We get downstream fifty feet or so and a shot is fired. We look back. The man is shooting at the target, not out over the river. Relief with a capital 'R'.

The man with the rifle brings to mind an incident that occurred last May. The club was paddling the Pine River in northeastern Wisconsin and there, too was a man walking along the shoreline. He was carrying a long-barreled revolver in his right hand down by his side. In all probability, it was not the same man that we heard shooting a few minutes ago. Back to the story that has no point... We kayakers greet the Wisconsin dude with the pistol and ask what he's up to. Thinking back, it's perhaps not the most brilliant question to ask of a guy with a gun in hand in the middle of the wilderness in northern Wisconsin. Anyway, the guy just gazes back like he had too much cheese for breakfast and then finally responds with absolutely no inflection in his voice, "Looking for stuff."

It was at that moment Luke developed an escape plan should he hear any shooting whatsoever. He would quickly point at me and yell something like, "He hates dairy products!" then roll his boat over and hide underneath with his head stuck up inside the air pocket of the cockpit, while drifting to a safe distance from the shooter. Not a bad plan except for one thing. The day we paddled the Pine River, the water was so low that it took all day to push, pull and drag the boats over more rocks than water in the thirteen miles traveled. And, in a river so shallow that ducks were wading rather than swimming, the possibility of a 6' 4" Luke hiding under his boat would be completely out of the question.

Now back to the story of the journey down the Mississippi, again that has no point... Not that the sun produced any positive effects throughout today's trip, but it has officially set. In the darkness ahead, we can hear a large flock of Canada Geese honking nervously as if sensing an invasion of their privacy, yet resisting the temptation to take to the air until confident security has indeed been breeched. It's like these enormous birds can't believe they are not alone on the water. Then again, in all likelihood we are the only four of the almost 5.2 million Minnesota residents out kayaking this frigid evening.

Brainerd's Lum Park is the take-out. Luke has gone ahead and somehow manages to cross the thirty feet of ice, and is safely on the beach in front of the playground. He is successful where the rest of us are not. Even paddling fast on the approach, the kayaks quickly slow as they slide across the ice toward shore. Each time, they come to a stop with dry land still out of reach. For reasons not easily understood, the boats then slide backwards into the water. After several failed attempts by the three in the water, Luke slides his boat back out on the ice while holding on to one end. Then each of us takes our turn grabbing onto the opposite end of his boat to be pulled onto the beach. Twenty-five tough miles have been logged in today.

When we arrive back in Grand Rapids shortly before 7:00, a heavy snow begins to fall. With winter setting in, paddling will be limited to the local waters around Grand Rapids until next spring when the trek south can be continued.

"Three grand essentials to happiness in this life are something to do, something to love, and something to hope for." -Joseph Addison, writer (1672–1719)

Trip Report
- 342.0 miles completed (14.8% of total trip)
- 1,965.0 to The Gulf

[2006]

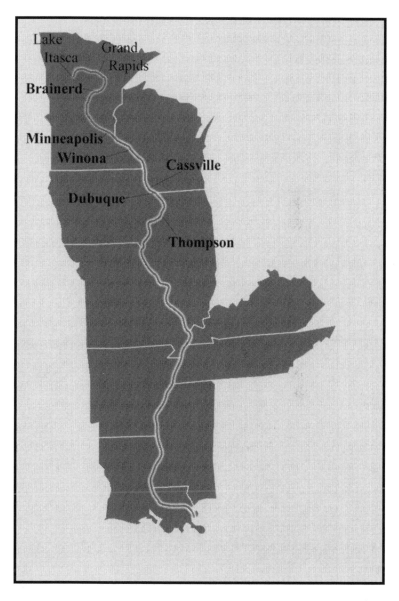

Lake Itasca
Grand Rapids
Brainerd
Minneapolis
Winona
Cassville
Dubuque
Thompson

Jim Lewis

2006 Introduction

The lakes in the Grand Rapids area freeze over every winter with ice, as much as three feet thick. There are, however, two sections of the Mississippi that remain mostly open through the cold months. One is four miles long. It is west of Grand Rapids, beginning at the Minnesota Power Access in Cohasset and ending at the Pokegama Dam. The other open water is an eight mile stretch from Steamboat Access in Grand Rapids to Itasca County 441 Access east of town. With that being said, the Itasca Kayakers were able to log in over four hundred miles as a group, getting on the water every week except one throughout the winter. The one week missed was scheduled and then cancelled at the last minute due to extenuating circumstances. Joan, however, showed up at the appointed time at the designated put-in that morning when no one else did. The teacher said, "I was going for perfect attendance." Over the winter, Joan was the only person who didn't miss an outing, no matter what the weatherman presented.

(Ready to paddle at a -17 F)

86

"Ka-Ka-Ska-Ska"

On February 18, 2006, the thermometer read a brisk -17 F with a reported wind chill of -25 F as the boats were unloaded at the Minnesota Power Landing. The river was at its best with thick steam rising from the water, then condensing and sculpting beautiful ice crystals of hoarfrost on the surrounding foliage.

Another highlight of the past winter took place on March 4 when five paddlers demonstrated extremely poor judgment allowing me to ramp up from my normal passive leadership style. I was getting tired of the same old stretches of river and was certain open water went well beyond the usual take-out of the eight mile route.

An excerpt from my journal...

March 4, 2006

There appears to be a lot of ice floating down the river at the 441 Access as we (Luke, Andy, Joan, Ana, Robin, and I) ready the kayaks. This raises my concern for what might be downstream, but I choose not to discuss it with the others. The first four-plus miles go well. The river is open and the snow covered landscape is truly awe-inspiring against the winter blue sky on this Saturday morning. It's the very reason why we're out here. We then come upon a field of ice closing off the river. Paddling the kayaks up on top of it, we traversed across using our homemade ice sticks made from 1" dowels and a lag screw sticking out the bottom. Luke portages through the woods instead, which proves to be a good choice. The ice is approximately a quarter-mile long and varies in thickness from less than a half-inch to several inches. We break through more than we stay on top. The trail broken by the lead boats quickly closes behind them in the river's current, and is of little or no use to those bringing up the rear. On the downstream side of the ice jam and back in open water, we encounter two Canada Geese, the only wildlife we see today.

We paddle a mile in open water and are faced with another ice field larger than the first. It is at the beginning of a sharp bend in the river so we all exit and drag our boats through the thick underbrush several hundred feet to where the river swings back in the opposite direction. Unfortunately, there is less than fifty yards of open water before we have to cross ice again. This crossing is relatively short, only fifteen to twenty yards, and thick enough to support us as we scoot across using our homemade ice sticks like ski poles.

Back in the water again and then out after just fifteen minutes of paddling – in again and then more ice and another long portage, slogging through thigh-deep snow along the river's edge. This time, at the re-entry point, we get in our boats. Using them as toboggans, we slide down the snow covered bank and across the ice making it all the way to the water without exerting what little energy we have left. Ten minutes later we are faced with more ice and lots of it. We are into hour-five of a trip that should have taken less than three hours. Luke breaks into the theme from "Gilligan's Island."

There is no arguing when we decide to exit a half mile upstream from our planned destination onto private property heavily posted with "NO TRESPASSING" signs. The land owner comes out to greet us as soon as we come into sight of his picture window. To say that he is less than excited to have uninvited company is an understatement. After we explain our predicament, his attitude changes and he is kind enough to let us leave our gear at the end of his driveway while Luke and I walk down the road to get the vehicles. This trip has displaced the trip taken on 1/9/2005 (upstream in a blizzard) for the most difficult winter outing. Though both grueling, I wouldn't have wanted to miss either one.

"**Take long walks in stormy weather or through deep snows in the fields and woods, if you would keep your spirits up. Deal with brute nature. Be cold and hungry and weary.**" -Henry David Thoreau, naturalist and author (1817–1862)

[Leg 6]

Brainerd, MN to St. Cloud, MN; 77.0 River Miles

Saturday, April 1, 2006

After a long winter's wait, we are at last back to our journey to the Gulf. Andy and I have both purchased new, longer boats for the bigger and faster water ahead. His is a red, seventeen-foot Current Designs Storm. Mine is the same, but white. We have also invested in more compact camping gear. It fits nicely into the watertight cargo holds of the boats. Included in the new gear are a few dry-bags, in a variety of sizes, used to protect our electronic equipment such as the cameras, MP3 players, and other items we want to make sure stay safe and dry.

Two-thirds of this leg will be done this weekend. The remainder will be put off for a week or so. The 8:30 launch this morning is from Evergreen Landing in Brainerd on the downstream side of the Potlatch Dam, the first dam since the Blandin Dam. The Mississippi River now enters an actual valley for the first time in the three hundred miles it has flowed thus far. The backdrop of swamps, lowland hardwoods and tamaracks, give way to red pine and mixed hardwoods.

Luke, Andy, Joan and I leave Grand Rapids at 6:15 to drive the ninety miles to the put-in. Four others join us there. The first two are members of the Itasca Kayakers, Troy Hilde and his thirteen year old son, Garrett from Foley, MN. The other two new paddlers are Linda Paige and Pete Voss. Although both are from Grand Rapids, they belong to another kayak club, the Brainerd Paddle Pushers. They have been kind enough to arrange the shuttling of the vehicles to the take-out at Fort Ripley Landing, twenty-one miles down stream.

Linda's cell phone rings while we are getting ready to launch. (It's her brother telling her that he had just played an April Fool's joke on their mom. He called mom and told her that Linda had already taken a spill into the river.) Linda shares the story, and goes on to say kayaking is similar to flying; if an accident is to happen, it will most likely be at either the take-off or landing. There is no mishap, however, at this put-in and all eight paddlers get underway safely. The current drifts us along toward our destination at 2.3 mph.

The waterfowl are plentiful. There are literally hundreds of Canadian Geese. Some are shy and fly at the first sight of the kayaks. Others linger for a curious look from along the shoreline. Flocks of golden-eye ducks fly over, making a distinctive whistling with every beat of the wing. The first loon of the season is spotted as it calls in response to the presence of the paddlers, then suddenly dives out of sight. A pair of trumpeter swans, North America's rarest native bird and also the largest (up to 45" long with a wingspan of 95" – practically the same size as a sheet of plywood), flies directly overhead on their trip north. The sound of the wind beneath their wings is a loud and steady WHOOMPH, WHOOMPH, WHOOMPH.

(Trumpeter Swan)

It's great to be on the river during spring migration. Before settlement of this area, the journals of river explorers Zebulon Pike, Lewis Cass, and Henry Schoolcraft all report incredible flocks of migratory birds and open plains where herds of buffalo grazed.

Still fifteen miles from Camp Ripley, we find that the birds aren't the only ones making noise. (Camp Ripley is now a National Guard training camp. It was originally built as Fort Gaines in 1848 to protect the Winnebago Indians, who were brought to Minnesota during treaty negotiations between the Dakota and Ojibwe to provide a buffer). The muffled sound of canon fire from Camp Ripley breaks through the solitude from time to time. Luke admits that at first the canon fire was mistaken for the drumming sound a ruffed grouse makes in the spring when the males defend their territory in hopes of attracting a mate. Disappointed to discover the truth, Luke had hoped to catch a glimpse of a giant grouse, perhaps tipping the scales around four hundred pounds.

Not knowing anything about the Brainerd kayak club, the Itasca Kayakers have a lot of questions for Linda and Pete. It is impressive to find out their club has taken part in trips to Alaska, Mexico, and Nova Scotia. And, once each summer, they have what they call a kayak rodeo. Among other games at the rodeo, they break into teams of two, and while out in the middle of the lake, they trade boats with one another. The objective is to do it without getting wet. During their local bi-weekly outings, they also do a great deal of rescue training. No one is allowed to paddle with the club unless they can successfully complete a wet exit and self rescue. I have to admit to them that most all members of the Itasca Kayakers would only be able to perform the wet exit portion of the entrance exam.

A picnic is on the slate today at Crow Wing State Park, access to the historic Red River Ox Cart Trail. The park is supposed to be eleven miles from the put-in. Linda says she has been there before, "It is just past a field on the left."

We know we are getting close. Up ahead a boat landing is on the left but there is no field. Actually, the area is completely grown over. Andy wants to know how many years it has been since Linda was here. "Well, it's been a while."

The best landing for a kayak appears to be adjacent to the concrete boat ramp on the downstream side. The grassy area provides an alternative to the concrete and will minimize the scraping and gouging of the boats' hulls. It looks treacherous, though. The river is about three feet deep right next to the narrow grassy shelf. It could mean trouble if the boat is not completely up on the grass. The first four boats make it okay. Linda is up next. I am following her, and ask that she wait until I get close enough to offer a hand to stabilize her. She does not respond, and continues the exit. Unfortunately, half-way out of the boat, she loses her balance and falls backwards into the river. Maybe this is why the Brainerd Paddle Pushers practice rescues so frequently. The secret of the Itasca Kayakers is not shared. (We take pride in practicing the art of staying in our boats.) Linda is wearing a wet suit and stays relatively dry even though she goes completely under. I wonder what her brother will say.

"Pete and Repeat went down to the river. Pete fell in. Who was left?" -Unknown.

On shore, Luke, who as you may recall is all over this sign reading business, spots one, "Picnic Area 1 mile→."

Back in the boats and another mile downstream, just past a field on the left, we find the picnic area with a landing much easier to negotiate. The fire built feels good against the cool spring air, especially for Linda. After much food, stories, and laughter, it's once more to the river.

Minutes later, Luke, Andy, Troy, and Garret are easily tempted by an ice float some forty feet long. They hop on the ice with their boats for a free ride. Andy convinces Garret to stand up in his boat for a quick photo. The current in this area is clocked at 3.2 mph and we make good time. The trip is going almost too fast.

❖ ❖ ❖

Eighteen miles of river is left behind when Linda and Pete, who have plans with family this evening, exit the river at her brother's house. It was good to have them along and everyone hopes they can join the Itasca Kayakers again soon.

Another hour passes and the rest of the gang find the vehicles at Fort Ripley Landing as planned. It's only 3:20. Had it been known that the river was this fast, more miles would have been scheduled. After loading the boats, we follow Troy to his house in Foley, not quite an hour's drive away. Troy and his wife, Mila, invited everyone to have dinner and stay with them tonight. It's a thousand times better than setting up tents, with rain in the forecast.

Chandra Parrish from Grand Rapids will be joining the group tomorrow. She arrives at Troy's late, after most have already called it a night. Chandra and her dad own and operate the local bike and ski shop in Grand Rapids. Not yet twenty-one, Chandra is a spirited people-person who enjoys working in retail, even though it cuts into her outdoor activities (cross country skiing, in-line skating, biking, and kayaking).

Sunday, April 2, 2006

It is 5:00, and no more or less than six alarm clocks signal the get-up. Joan doesn't bother with a light before she begins readying for the day. She is unaware of Chandra sleeping on the floor with her head directly in the flight path to the bathroom. It's good for Chandra that she has been blessed with a hard head and a soft heart capable of forgiveness.

"I think there is only one quality worse than hardness of heart, and that is softness of head." -Theodore Roosevelt, 26th US President (1858–1919)

After a big breakfast, we step out into an uncomfortable 37 F predawn darkness and a steady rain. No one complains. It's just the way it is. Sometimes, you're the bug; sometimes, you're the windshield.

At 8:00, we are on schedule and at the same location we took out yesterday. Goodbyes are said to Mila and Kirsten, the fourth Hilde, who have come along to shuffle the cars. Garret chose to sleep in leaving six kayakers (Luke, Andy, Joan, Chandra, Troy, and me).

Depending upon who is discussing the rain, and when, it is described as: a drizzle, sprinkles, and even simply rain. The intensity at each of the levels is branded as: lightly, mediumly, and heavily. The one thing everyone agrees on is that it remains constant and it continues throughout the entire twenty-five miles of today's voyage, accumulating a little less than a half-inch. The headwind varies from calm to 12 mph. On the positive side, today's current is 5.0 mph for the first ten miles.

The section of river below Camp Ripley is known as Thousand Islands – islands created by log jams during the 19th century. The largest log jam in the world was formed north of Little Falls in 1893–94. It extended over six miles, measuring a half-mile wide and thirty to sixty feet deep. An estimated 4.5 billion board feet of lumber was caught in the jam and it took one hundred fifty men, five teams of horses, and one steam engine about six months to break it up. Logs left behind gathered sediment and eventually became the islands they are today.[3]

There is confusion regarding the location of the portage as we arrive in Little Falls, MN at the Little Falls Dam at 11:30, eight miles short of the scheduled take-out. I forgot to bring the map, but I believe there is a good chance that the portage is on river-left. The sign, "DANGER-DAM AHEAD-KEEP OUT" in one foot high letters in five locations across the face of the MN Hwy 27 Bridge fifty yards upstream from the dam fails to provide much of a hint. To the left is a fence that is at least five feet high. We go to the right. No indication of a portage there either. Some things can't wait so Chandra, Joan, Troy, and Andy exit on the grassy shoreline and race each other to the gas station down the street to meet a variety of needs.

Meanwhile, Luke returns to river-left to explore the downstream side of the bridge, nearer the dam, in hope of finding a way to portage. I remain behind on the right side of the river to watch the gear for the others. Twenty minutes later, the gas station bunch returns. On a side trip over the bridge, they found that Luke has discovered the secret passage around the dam, beyond the "KEEP OUT" warning.

I paddle over to where Luke is spotted, and following his lead, manage a safe exit onto the bridge apron. The other four carry their boats across the bridge adding an additional hundred yards to the already three hundred twenty-five yard portage. After an hour of hauling boats and gear to the downstream side of the dam, it's time for lunch.

Next to the river is a park-like setting with paved walkways, freshly pruned shrubs and mature oak trees full of restless buds. Across the walking trail that follows the river's edge is a well maintained assisted living facility. Rain continues to fall in a "mediumly" drizzle as we catch our breath and eat lunch at a nearby picnic table. There is a mutual hope that those passing by would stop staring, take pity, and offer up coupons for free pizza, Starbuck's coffee or something. No such luck. There is also talk of sending Chandra (who won the "Okay, show us your most pathetic look" contest) over to knock on a window and ask for cookies. We dismiss the idea thinking the residents may be in after-Sunday-morning-church nap mode.

The re-entry to the river does not come without challenge. There is a sharp and slippery two foot wide concrete ledge a few inches above the surface of the water. In the river are various size rocks and boulders exposed and hidden, then exposed again in the torrent of water below the open gates of the dam. A fifteen foot standing wave at the base of the dam watches over the turbulence like a medieval gargoyle. Troy assists me in getting my boat in the river first. The plan is to have me positioned in the river to help others. Unfortunately, I am caught in the eddy current and drawn upstream towards the dam before I can get control. It's a struggle to get turned about without being drawn to the swiftness of the main flow. Meanwhile, the others seem oblivious to my fight and continue with their own launch. The only help I can offer is "Point your boat downstream, paddle hard and don't look back!" Everyone makes it safely.

There's an elevation drop of over a hundred feet in the next seventeen miles, but the dams take all the fun out of what could be an exceptionally good ride. There are only three miles of strong current before the river slows to virtually nothing as it enters the reservoir five miles above Blanchard Dam, today's take-out. At the landing, there's a small build up of ice along shore, but nothing posing any serious problems.

We are headed for home at 3:00, looking forward to a hot cup of coffee at the first gas station in route.

"Nothing is worth more than this day." -Goethe

Wednesday, April 12, 2006

Ten days since the last trip and it's back to the Blanchard Dam. Troy is waiting when Andy, Luke, Joan, and I arrive at 9:00, an hour late. The extra hour has given Troy a chance to scout out the best access. Rather than having to take the five hundred yard portage, he has found a narrow dirt road leading to the lower side of the dam instead. Clearly, Troy is much better at reconnaissance than I am!

The put-in below Blanchard Dam, the largest hydroelectric dam on the upper Mississippi, is well away from the major tumult, but there is still plenty of wave action to pound the boats against the rocks in the shallow water as each one is launched.

As we are overdressed for the 54 F the first layer of clothing comes off within thirty minutes of starting the trip. The forecast is for a high in the upper 60s with an 8–10 mph tail wind developing around noon. It's going be a good day.

A mile south of the dam is the MacDougall Homestead, now owned and maintained by the Nature Conservancy. Atop the sixty foot bluff is a heron rookery. At river level, an unbelievable number of ducks and geese border the shore like parade goers lined up to watch fancy floats, however, it is not certain if their endless squawking is intended to applaud the kayakers' progress, or a means to communicate a warning to feathered friends downriver. Roughly two-thirds of all North American migratory birds use the Mississippi corridor as their route each spring and fall.

The travel itinerary calls for paddling fifteen miles before stopping at Stearns County Park for lunch. Travel time is no more than two and a half hours. While we are seated at a picnic table overlooking the river eating lunch, the first powerboat of the season is seen making its maiden spring voyage – a subtle reminder that the river is not reserved for only quiet sports. It won't be long before we will be sharing the waterway with other crafts and barges in greater numbers than we care to think about. The usual hour passes before, "It's time. Break's over."

The next hurdle is the Champion International Paper Company Dam nine miles away in Sartell, MN. The current is slower now and the nine miles takes two hours. To pass time, we discuss the homes along the river – very large pricey homes.

"Being rich is having money; being wealthy is having time." -Stephen Swid, executive

It's interesting to see the wide variety of stair designs used to gain river access from dwellings situated high upon the banks. Stair steps, numbering close to a hundred or even more, made of wood, steel, or concrete twist across the frontage. Some of them have small built-in rest areas. Other staircases extend straight as an arrow up the hillside providing every opportunity possible for cardiac arrest.

The wind has developed as predicted. Unfortunately, the wind is not from the northwest and not at our backs. It is coming from the southwest, more of a headwind, and definitely not 8–10 mph. Using my anemometer, I measure the wind velocity to be in excess of 17 mph.

The paper mill is on river-left in Sartell. The three hundred yard portage around the dam begins on the right, next to the street. The method found to work best when doing portages such as this is to take two boats of equal length side by side with one person at each end. Troy and I make up one team.

Luke and Andy are the other. Joan latches onto the fifth boat and drags it about half the distance of the portage, which is as far as the grass boulevard extends before turning to asphalt.

Troy and I continue past a little wayside rest and the River Depot, a friendly looking pub on the corner. The put-in is at the bottom of a steep fifty foot incline, well away from the dam's discharge. Someone has strategically placed flat rocks down the face of the hill to provide steps, making the task a bit easier. Even so, one boat is left at the top of the hill for a second trip. Luke and Andy follow suit. After our second boat, Troy and I return to help Joan with hers. The temperature is in the lower seventies and much too warm to be making a portage this long.

After we're all on the river and Sartell is a shrinking image over our shoulders, Joan announces, "I think those guys would have bought us all a beer."

Her four male travelling companions look at her in surprise and ask in unison, "What guys?!"

It took a while to get the whole story out of her... While the boats were being lugged down the hillside, Joan, still wearing her life jacket and spray skirt, slipped away to the River Depot. The conversation inside:

"I suppose you're looking for the bathroom." [Very perceptive for a guy spending the afternoon in the bar drinking.]

"Yes."

"Where you coming from?" is the next question when Joan returns.

"We started at Lake Itasca."

"Where you going?"

"The Gulf." [Interest peaks]

A barrage of other questions follow, including one from the bartender lady, "Do you work?"

"I'm on spring break."

"Ka–Ka–Ska–Ska"

Another volley of questions and answers follow. Joan knew it was time to make her way to the door – not because her friends are waiting, but because one of the guys in the bar thought she should arm wrestle his buddy.

Lessons learned… First, don't let Joan wander off into a bar by herself. Secondly, you may or may not get offered free beer if you wear your life jacket and spray skirt into a bar. (Luke and Andy say they will experiment with this at another time – perhaps after work one day next week.)

Andy and I are lagging a couple hundred yards behind the others as we get about three miles downstream from Sartell. Andy turns to me and mentions he can hear the sound of fast water. Looking ahead we see some bubbling action in the river. Joan is out in the lead when she suddenly drops completely out of sight. Andy and I then see Luke drop out of sight, followed by Troy. I turn to Andy, "Perhaps we should have looked at the map closer."

We're at Heim's Mill Access, located at the confluence of the Sauk and Mississippi Rivers. Had the map been checked, we would have found the following notation: "**Caution:** *Rapids below the confluence with the Sauk are ranked as Class I to Class III. A portage trail is available along the city park on the left bank. Scout before proceeding.*"

"Oh."

"*Facts do not cease to exist because they are ignored.*"
-Aldous Huxley, novelist (1894–1963)

As I am fast approaching the three foot rock shelf, I realize my camera is not secured inside the dry-bag, which is inside my unzipped deck bag. I have only enough time to reach down and zip the deck bag shut before going over. Like with the others, the waves completely engulf the front half of my boat at the drop and again a few more times before entering more calm waters. Like the others, I am successful at negotiating the hundred yards of rapids which are definitely approaching Class III today. The camera survives too.

We reach St. Cloud thirty miles from this morning's put-in, at 4:00 after averaging 4.3 mph today including the breaks and portage.

Trip Report
-   419.0 miles completed (18.2% of total trip)
-   1,888.0 to The Gulf

[Leg 7]

St. Cloud, MN to Minneapolis, MN; 71.3 River Miles

Saturday, May 19, 2006

It's more than a three hour drive from Grand Rapids to the put-in below the St. Cloud Dam. People begin to arrive at my house before 6:00 am. Joan is the first, and hardly out of the car, when she asks "Are there any portages today?"

As I reply, "Not today," I can't help but notice Joan's look of disappointment. Perhaps she's been having second thoughts about declining the challenge to arm wrestling at the River Depot in Sartell on the last trip and is hoping for another similar opportunity.

The objective today is to paddle the twenty-nine miles from St. Cloud, MN to Monticello, MN and camp at Ellison Park. Camping at Ellison Park is not normally allowed, but after a few phone calls a month ago, I was able to connect with the right people and was given permission. The city agreed to even provide extra patrol through the night.

The cast of players (eleven this time) converging at the put-in at 9:30 include Troy Hilde and his son, Garrett, returning for their second performance, Annette Albertson, (Andy's sister), her boyfriend, Scott Krohn, Chuck King, and Jeff Haugen who are all from the Minneapolis area. Andy, Luke, Joan, and I brought along Ron Ulseth I, a sixty-two year young retired school teacher from Grand Rapids. Traci, spouse of Luke, is playing the role of "ground support." She will deliver the camping gear to the park and make sure a vehicle is at the take-out tomorrow afternoon in Minneapolis.

Once all are on the water safely, Joan takes off like a greyhound dog chasing a mechanical rabbit. I'm not sure what she ate for breakfast, but I know it wasn't biscuits and gravy. The rest of the gang does not catch up to her for nine miles and then only because she stopped to wait.

This is great countryside. The river is several hundred feet wide with bluffs ranging from fifty to a hundred feet in height and hundreds of small islands along the way, some over a mile long. Though much of the river bank is undeveloped, it is only matter of time before progress will bring more dense population. The moderate sized cities of St. Cloud and Anoka were once mere trading posts built by trappers and traders, the first white men to travel the river.

Clearwater is twelve miles south from the put-in. According to a friend of Troy's, who has paddled a canoe from St. Cloud to Clearwater on a few occasions, the trip usually takes three hours. We arrive in two, due to the current varying from 4–6.5 mph. Then we continue past the city making great progress, and yet we seem to have plenty of time to enjoy each other's company and the wildlife. The weather isn't too bad either. Earlier, there was an hour or so of light rain, but when it edged closer to "mediumly," we put on rain gear and within minutes the rain stopped all together. We should have thought of it earlier.

After twenty miles of paddling, everyone is looking forward to lunch at the Oak Island campsite. Unfortunately, the site is already taken by some other river folk. We paddle on another two miles to Snuffies Landing near the city of Becker, MN and stop there instead.

"Ka-Ka-Ska-Ska"

Content after a fill of cold sandwiches, chips, trail mix, and a variety of candy, there is no doubt that we can make it the last seven miles without starving. On the water again, I break out the trivia cards. Holding onto each other's boats, we gather into one large flotilla. Joan is out front doing the necessary paddling to keep us in the channel while the rest of the group is playing the game. She is comfortable in this task and would rather not be part of the game anyway. Joan spends a lot of her time at school playing games with the kids. "Off work, I would rather eat a greasy polish sausage on a white bun than play another game." And we know that's not going to happen.

(Getting the flotilla going)

As the flotilla approaches the MN Hwy. 25 Bridge, it is plain to see that the current is too much for eleven kayaks to

continue on safely as a "barge." If we want to successfully negotiate the opening under the bridge, we'll have to split off quickly and go at it independently. We let go of each other and grab
the paddles, but not quickly enough. The distance between the
kayaks and the bridge diminishes in a blink of an eye. We enter
the trough still grouped too tight in a bunch to paddle with any
effectiveness. The current has more control of the boats than we
have. Jeff is the last one to enter the chute and with the others
directly in front of him, he is given no chance whatsoever. His
boat swings around sideways catching the bridge strut mid-
ship spilling him and his gear into the river. By now, his com-
padres have been spit out the downstream side and are almost
instantaneously thirty to fifty yards ahead.

*"If everyone is thinking alike then somebody isn't think-
ing."* -George Smith Patton III, U.S. Army General
(1885–1945)

Half of us turn about and struggle against the river's power
to go to Jeff's aid, retrieving a dry-bag here, a sandal there, and
other stuff found floating in between. Ten minutes later, Jeff is
back in his boat with bilge pump pumping and happy to find
that the only thing lost was his pride. He is willing to wait for
dry clothes until we arrive at today's final destination a half-
mile downstream.

There are several families at the park visiting this Saturday afternoon. Perhaps it's a coincidence, but they all leave the park
abruptly minutes after we show up. Perchance their fun time
has ended. Or it could be they overhear someone in the kayak

group mention something about deploying the "Naked Sandwich," though Andy quickly declares it will not be required.

After camp is set up, it's a trip to Hawk's Sport's Bar for dinner. We spend the remainder of the evening sitting around the campfire telling stories.

Sunday, May 20, 2006

Though the overnight temperature dipped to the mid-thirties, most everyone slept well. I am the first to greet the new day at 6:00. A light fog lay suspended above the river. Families of Canada Geese walk their broods down to water's edge for a peek into what the near future will bring. Sounds of song birds fill the air as our camp begins to stir into life.

Brock Carlson, Luke's stepbrother from Minneapolis, joins the lineup this morning but three others (Jeff, Scott and Annette) who have other plans for today leave for home. Our boats are in the water at 9:30 and we are off to the big city. It is thirty-two crow-fly miles, but an additional ten river miles to the take-out at the Plymouth Bridge in downtown Minneapolis. The river's current is well over 5 mph, again making for excellent paddling. Two and a half-hours later and sixteen miles down stream, it's a twenty minute stop to stretch our legs and have a snack.

Another hour of paddling passes before we enter an eight mile stretch of wildlife refuge which ends on the upstream side of Elk River, MN. A more beautiful section of river for a refuge would be hard to find. Close attention is paid to the GPS as we weave our way around the many islands. This is not to save time but to take advantage of the scenic shore line and the majestic oaks that lean out over the water to provide a canopy of protection against the heat of the sun.

Five miles short of our portage around the Coon Rapids Dam, someone on shore at Point Park is yelling "Welcome to Coon Rapids Itasca Kayakers!!!" At the same time, a pontoon boat is fast approaching from downstream. I paddle over to the shore to find out who wants our attention there. Andy turns toward the pontoon boat. Someone on board the pontoon asks Andy if Luke McLeod is amongst the group. It's Traci's family who thought it would be fun to intercept the kayaks. On shore, the same Jeff who paddled with our group yesterday, and his wife have been out for a bike ride. By coincidence, they arrive at the park as we come into view. It's always good to have friends in far away places.

"A single rose can be my garden... a single friend, my world." -Leo Buscaglia, author, speaker and professor (1924–1998)

Lunch is at 2:15 at the Coon Rapids Dam before making the one hundred fifty yard portage. This is the easiest portage so far, thanks to Chuck's wife. She showed up with her car, to assist in transporting the gear around the dam while we carry the empty boats across the wide open grassy field. The hour passes quickly, and we're back on the water with a little more than twelve miles to the final take-out for the day. The sound of birds singing is now drowned out by the drone of power boats, air traffic, and nearby highway noise. We have entered a different world.

"Solitude is painful when one is young, but delightful when one is more mature." -Albert Einstein, theoretical physicist and Nobel Prize winner (1879–1955)

❖ ❖ ❖

"Ka-Ka-Ska-Ska"

This afternoon is a series of "firsts." We see our first barge moored alongside of the river. It's loaded with gravel, waiting for a tug to help it back downstream. Andy rams his boat into the side of the barge telling me, "I took on the first one. The rest will be up to you." We also pass under our first freeway, then the first glimpse of the Minneapolis sky line from the river. There is no doubt. It is exciting to be entering the city by kayak. Groupies are a first, as well. People, dining on an outside patio of a restaurant, shout an uplifting hello and take our picture as we paddle by. Luke complains that he is tired of all the attention and wishes that the paparazzi would just go away.

(Entering the big city)

Traci is at the Plymouth Bridge in downtown Minneapolis at 5:15 when we arrive. According to the GPS, the river has dropped another seventy-two feet in altitude from this morning's put-in and we have averaged 5.4 mph including breaks.

Trip Report
- – 490.3 miles completed (21.3% of total trip)
- – 1,816.7 to The Gulf

[Leg 8]

Minneapolis, MN to Winona, MN; 126.3 River Miles

Saturday, July 8, 2006

The group drove down from Grand Rapids last evening and spent the night at Jeff Haugen's home in a northern Minneapolis suburb. Luke and Tony are not along on this trip and will have to paddle this section later. There are five paddlers doing this leg of the river: Andy Albertson, Ron Ulseth I, Joan Bibeau, Harvey Frisco and, of course, me. Harvey at 71 is the envy of many. He's loved the outdoors since he was a youngster growing up in Amsterdam. Spending the bulk of his career in Oregon, he has climbed all the major peaks in the Pacific Northwest. At retirement, he moved to Minnesota which is without saying mountain-poor but water-rich, so it was time to change gears and experience the area by kayak. In the winter, Harvey enjoys the endless miles of groomed cross country ski trails in the area.

"Live as if you were living a second time, and as though you had acted wrongly the first time". -Viktor Frankl, author, neurologist and psychiatrist, Holocaust survivor (1905–1997)

Ron's van and the trailer are left at a friend's house near the put-in at the Plymouth Bridge in downtown Minneapolis. We are on the river at 10:15 with a slight rain falling, confident the front will quickly pass and is not worthy of the magic rain gear.

❖ ❖ ❖

We are inside the lock on the upside of St. Anthony Falls, after thirty-five minutes of paddling. The lockmaster finds out it is our first time to lock through and says, "As long as you guys are in here alone, go ahead and paddle around. Enjoy it."

About six million gallons of water is required to fill this lock chamber for each lockage – accomplished in roughly eight minutes. We are pleased to find out there is no turbulence while entering or departing the locks. The only discomfort is the smell of dead fish. It doesn't take many dead fish on the ride with you in a confined space to make eight minutes seem way too long. We assume the reason for the dead fish is that most people in the area catch and release. Eating fish caught in this section of the river more than once per month is not recommended due to the high level of contamination.

(The first lock)

"Ka-Ka-Ska-Ska"

The river drops one hundred thirteen feet between here and the next three locks: Lower St. Anthony Falls, Lock & Dam No. 1 in Minneapolis, and Lock & Dam No. 2 in Hastings located forty miles downstream.

Two hours and two locks behind us, we consider ourselves much more than novices at this lock business. Practically a mile upstream from Lock & Dam No. 1, Andy uses his marine radio tuned to channel 14 to ask for southbound passage. The lockmaster assures him it will be ready in fifteen minutes – much better than having to wait until getting there and pulling the signal rope.

Two miles below Lock & Dam No. 1, the bawling of bagpipes can be heard drifting down off the bluff from Old Fort Snelling. The fort was built in 1819 and the country was changed forever. The first steamboat to reach St. Paul was the Virginia in 1823. Soon the Native American tribes of the Dakota and the Ojibwe were purged from their homelands. Dams were built to yoke the power of St. Anthony Falls for industrial use in the milling of grain and textiles. Steamers brought freight, settlers, and visitors to the small but fast growing towns of St. Anthony Falls and Pig's Eye. Later, these towns became communities of greater Minneapolis and St. Paul.

We paddle another hour downstream. Under the Interstate 35E overpass, the sound of motor traffic above is deafening. We might as well be on the tarmac at the international airport.... "The fort was built and the country was changed forever."

By early afternoon, the sky is clear of any clouds. This evidently sends an invitation to everyone who owns a power boat to get out on the river, go as fast as you can and likewise, see how much noise can be made. Unending waves roll across the river in every direction recoiling back and forth between the channel and the shore. The two foot waves of one boat catch Harvey, who is paddling closer to shore than he probably should be, and propel him up on the rocks. As he pitches back and forth to get free, heartlessly the same boat returns for another shot at him. This time Harvey takes a sizeable wave over the side. Even with his spray skirt in place, he gets soaked but somehow remains upright and is washed off the rocks with the reflection wave from shore.

"The weak can never forgive. Forgiveness is the attribute of the strong." -Mohandas K. Gandhi (1869–1948)

The lunch we had along the riverbank at the St. Paul City Park is beginning to wear off three hours later. I hail down a power boat and ask if there's a place nearby where we can get something to eat. "Yep, a marina less than a mile downstream on the left."

Two miles further, I ask another boater, "Straight ahead, about a half-mile on your left."

We're getting closer. Another mile is behind us and a third boater is consulted, "Around the next corner and on the right."

Sure enough, there it is and to our surprise, the guy I talked with first, is sitting at the next table. (If we had only been aware at this time how few people can actually provide precise directions, we would have stopped asking – like virtually all our male counterparts on this earth who apparently have already learned this lesson in life.)

"History is a vast early warning system." -Norman Cousins, editor and author (1915–1990)

After supper we paddle until 9:15 before setting up camp on an island twenty-seven river miles from this morning's starting point. To our dismay, it is no more than two crow-fly miles from the South St. Paul Municipal Airport. And though we have been paddling in the metro area all day, we were seldom aware of it except for when going under the bridges. The city has been successful in keeping most of the shoreline of the river in its natural state creating perfect habitat for eagles, ospreys, red-tailed hawks, falcons, great blue herons, egrets, and a variety of song birds.

(A great blue heron)

The tent sites are at the top of a steep sugar sand rise from the beach. Our feet sink well beyond ankle deep, with each step to the crest. We try not to make too many trips back to the boats. The final hour before turning in is spent sharing stories around a campfire, glad that Joan listened to her mother and brought lots of popcorn.

Sunday, July 9, 2006

Soon after a comparatively early start at 8:10, Andy and I locate a shortcut through a backwater. We hope to avoid boat traffic, and at the same time, get to see some of the river seldom seen by anyone. The backwater, however, is too shallow to paddle and we're too far into it to turn around. It's knuckles pushing in the hard sand bottom, propelling the kayaks an inch or two at a time, instead of paddling. When we tire of this, we step out and pull our boats to deeper water and the main channel.

Mid-morning, I paddle over to inspect a house boat moored along shore that is proudly flying the Jolly Roger. It is obvious the vessel is of custom design, about twelve feet wide and perhaps twenty-four feet long, floating on two very mismatched and well used aluminum pontoons. The deck and cabin are a patchwork quilt of various sizes and shapes of plywood and other materials. Two canoes lashed alongside are most likely there to be available as life boats.

"Everything should be made as simple as possible, but not simpler." -Albert Einstein, theoretical physicist and Nobel Prize winner (1879–1955)

I approach the 'pirate ship' and a young man in his twenties, looking as interesting as his yacht, comes out on the forward deck to greet me. It turns out this guy and ten of his friends will be taking this thing downstream in September, hoping to be in New Orleans by Christmas. He and I exchange a few river experiences before I realize my traveling companions are nearly out of sight, and it's time to go. "Good-bye and good luck!"

"Ka-Ka-Ska-Ska"

Fifteen miles and more than five hours from the put-in this morning finds our kayaks parked at the upstream side of Lock & Dam No. 2. We have a forty-five minute wait due to northbound traffic. A short portage around the spillway is a consideration. In light of the temperature sitting at 85 F and no clouds to give relief from the sun, we choose to stay in the boats tucked up close to the concrete barrier in the only shade seen all day. The downtime is used to make calls home giving progress reports. Lunch will wait another hour or so when we arrive at Prescott, WI.

Andy and I are the first to arrive at Prescott, the point of confluence of the Mississippi and the St. Croix. The other three are not far behind. It is crazy time! The volume of boat traffic experienced so far on the river seems minimal to what we face here. The inlet to the St. Croix is packed with boats of all shapes and sizes motoring along, going from one river to the other and back again. Two sheriff's deputies on jet skis and another two in a runabout are patrolling the area.

As Andy and I approach the front of the small service station along the river, we are asked to pull up in one of the empty slips off to the side. Inside the service station, we are glad that cold beer is sold in singles and even more glad to find that we can drink while we shop. Wisconsin is a good place to be.

Sitting on the dock, we munch on chips and eat "Made Fresh" gas station sandwiches – the first to have ever passed Joan's lips. We north-woods paddlers sit in awe of the circus activity before us. The sheriff's boats stop people at random checking for safety gear, registration and who knows what. Andy questions, "Are the bikini girls sitting on the bow of these boats standard features or options, costing extra?" There's a lot of discussion and opinions, but no one knows for sure.

Keeping the stop to the standard sixty minutes, we reluctantly leave the 'festival of fools' and shove off.

❖ ❖ ❖

After eight more miles, we stop for a quick break on shore. Getting back on the river is tricky business due to large waves created by the power boats' blended wakes. Ron and Harvey make it right away, but Andy catches a huge wave broadside slamming his rudder into the rocks, dousing his radio, camera, and telephone. When the tsunami withdraws, Andy discovers a minnow in his lap.

With Andy's boat pumped dry and his wet shorts stowed on the rear deck under the bungee, and his rudder held in place with a piece of parachute cord, another attempt at launching is made. It's a success.

"Failure is only the opportunity to begin again more intelligently." -Henry Ford, U.S. industrialist and automobile manufacturer (1863–1947)

The intent is to find a private campground with showers in Red Wing, MN, slightly less than ten river miles away. Not all the other boats on the river today are large screaming machines. There are a few small fishing boats and canoes among them. One small fishing boat is commanded by Don Janson. He and Andy hit it off and Andy ends up with Don's last cold beverage.

Later, Andy and I come alongside a canoe. The couple in the canoe has been paddling the Cannon River today and are nearing the end of their trip. We enjoy the company of the couple for more than a mile before going our separate ways. "Do you think they knew I was paddling in my underwear?"

"We'll never know for sure."

"Ka-Ka-Ska-Ska"

Thirty-five miles have been logged in today as the kayaks make the last bend before entering Red Wing an hour before dark. It is not easy to find a campground and we explorers are sure that lesser sailors would have given up. Perhaps we should have, too. The elusive campground is located next to a frequently traveled railroad bridge, downwind from the city's waste treatment facility, and across from some sort of heavy industry producing a low-frequency but steady and annoying hum. Though the grounds are fairly well kept, it seems that the trash collection schedule has been ignored for the past several weeks. The overflowing dumpsters and cans which are corralled behind a high green stockade fence give off the unique scent of decaying fish and rotting food. We select a tent site located as far from it all as possible, near another tent camper. Our neighbor is a tall and skinny, twenty-something guy from upstate New York, who has finished his last day of biking west. Tomorrow, he will catch a bus home. JC is his name. However, if you ask Joan, she'll tell you his name is RW or CM or DJ or some other two-letter combination. She claims she has difficulty remembering unusual names when subjected to extreme temperatures. (Joan's exposure, not the names.)

The sun has been down for quite a while before we take off on foot to find supper. JC recommends a Jamaican restaurant two blocks away. We worn travelers enter, find a table, get seated, and are told the kitchen closed forty-five minutes earlier. The waitress reads the letdown on our faces and says she'll be right back. Ten minutes later she returns with plates of jerk chicken, salad, rice and beans, set out in family style. She says that's all she could find. She returns again ten minutes later and claims she can also produce ice cream if anyone desires. There are two takers.

It's 11:00 when we bid each other goodnight.

Monday, July 10, 2006

Today is Andy's birthday. He and Joan are the first ones ready. They paddle across the river into town to get coffee for the troops. At 8:20, the kayaks are headed south.

A mile downstream, a decision is made to take a route around the backside of an island that seems to have good flow. (Looking back now, it was probably my idea.) Unfortunately, as we round the far end of the mile-long island to return to the main channel, the kayaks run aground on a sand bar. We are once again forced to exit the boats and drag them a few hundred yards to deeper water. Lessons learned – do not take short cuts and do not to listen to Jim.

(Walking when we should be paddling)

The next challenge is Lake Pepin, three miles wide and twenty-one miles long. Water skiing was invented here on this

"Ka-Ka-Ska-Ska"

water in 1922 by an adventurous youth who was sometimes pulled by an airplane.

The 10–12 mph headwind is relatively kind but Andy is a bit disappointed he cannot use his sail. Over the last two days, he's managed to get out of paddling quite a few miles. Andy has a new sail he designed out of PVC tubing and rip-stop nylon.

"The pessimist complains about the wind; the optimist expects it to change; the realist adjusts the sails." -William Arthur Ward, college administrator, writer (1921–1994)

The city of Pepin is reached after a long, hot eight hours. We are greeted on the beach near the Pepin Yacht Club by Brian and Maryann. The two have been monitoring our approach from inside the clubhouse for the last mile or so. Somehow they knew a cold beer would be greatly appreciated. It's always a joy to meet psychics. For the next thirty minutes, stories are traded with our new friends. The last words of advice from Brian and Maryann are "There's a little marina downstream called Slippery's. Be sure to stop there."

We leave lakeside and hike up the hill to Paul and Fran's Grocery for supplies. Using up all of the last thirty minutes allowed before getting back on the river, we buy groceries, eat today's breakfast, lunch and supper.

Six miles and two more hours of paddling after Lake Pepin, "Do we want to stop at Slippery's?" Foolish question – the stop is deserved.

A guy named Brian and his nine-year old son, Jordan, happen down to the dock to visit. The father-son team has dozens of questions for us about the boats and the journey. After very little coaxing, I convince Jordan to give kayaking a try. Joan volunteers her boat and with me at his side, Jordan paddles out into the river, then down the face of the marina and back. Having never paddled before, the young lad does an awesome job. Jordan's voyage lasts only ten minutes, but what a smile! While Jordan and I were out paddling, Jordan's dad got a round of drinks for the group.

"To give pleasure to a single heart by a single kind act is better than a thousand head-bowings in prayer." -Saadi, poet (c. 1200 AD)

There is less than forty minutes of daylight left after leaving Slippery's. Andy, checking our location on his GPS, is surprised to find we are parallel with Albertson Slough. I tell him it is his birthday gift. "We wanted to buy you a star named in your honor, but they were too expensive."

As night falls, head lamps are deployed and bugs are attracted in massive swarms. Heat, bugs, and darkness make for an uncomfortable state of affairs. At 10:00, Andy contacts Lock & Dam No. 4 located at Alma, WI, fifteen minutes downstream.

Once through the lock, we make a hard right into a backwater channel. We find a small peninsula that is a very suitable campsite. It's 11:00 when the five tents are pitched, spread across a hundred feet of flat sand beach, inches above the water. After more than an hour of throwing peanut shells into the fire, we settle in for the night.

Tuesday, July 11, 2006

Joan and I are the first ready today. The city of Alma is less than a mile away so we paddle back upstream to get breakfast for everyone. The local convenience store offers up tasty egg and sausage sandwiches, hot coffee, and orange juice. Back at camp, time is taken to eat before getting underway.

(View from backwater campsite below Alma)

Leaving camp, the backwater channel past an island is like a powerful magnet. There is no way we can resist the tempting shortcut, only to discover one more time the water is too low for paddling. Once again, we are compelled to drag the boats down the Mighty Mississippi. Ho. Hum.

Rain begins to fall around 9:00. When it turns into a downpour, we resort to rain gear — not to protect ourselves from getting wet as it's already too late for that. Instead, we figure that once we go through the hassle of getting the gear from where it is stowed and go through the balancing act to get suited up while floating down the river, it'll stop raining. Sure enough, the rain stops within fifteen minutes.

Between the mid-week reduction in pleasure craft and minimal barge traffic, it's easy to maintain a 3.5 mph average. For whatever reason, we have seen less than a half dozen barges since this leg of the river began last Saturday. Though considerably slower, barges are far more energy efficient than rail or truck. The most interesting barge is the one that is coming upriver at this time. The US Army Corps of Engineers is pushing what looks like a standard single barge container, usually one hundred ninety-five feet long and thirty-five feet wide. Trailing alongside of the tow and barge container is a smaller power boat. Then about a hundred yards out in front of us paddlers, the barge and towboat stop, turn completely around, and head back downstream. The smaller power boat continues upriver, but not before it uses an onboard water pump and a high-pressure and high-volume nozzle to give those on the barge a good soaking. The barge crew shakes it off with laughs and waves at the crew on the smaller boat. I can't explain it – just reporting the event.

"War will exist until that distant day when the conscientious objector enjoys the same reputation and prestige that the warrior does today." -John F. Kennedy, 35th US president (1917–1963)

On the upper Mississippi, a single towboat with engines producing 3,000 to 4,000 horsepower can push a maximum of fifteen loaded barges – five tied together end to end and three abreast at speeds from 3.5–11 mph. The same volume of commodities carried on the fifteen barges would require a train three miles long or a convoy of eight hundred seventy semi-trucks. The river below St. Louis, MO is deeper and has less change in elevation so locks and dams are no longer necessary. On the deeper and slower part of the river, towboat engines put out 8,000 to 10,000 horsepower and will typically push as many as forty to sixty barges per tow. (A tow consists of one towboat and one or more barges depending on the cargo.) The cargo could be grain, chemicals, petroleum products, scrap iron, sand, coal, or just about anything. A barge load of wheat is enough to make 2.25 million loaves of bread.

After paddling fourteen miles since breakfast, Lock & Dam No. 5 is in sight and Andy calls ahead. Locking through goes well and paddling resumes in no time at all. Nearing Winona, we see the bluffs beyond the backwaters are getting higher, reaching almost three hundred feet. Wildlife continues to be bountiful, especially fish. Each of us has had our own experience with fish jumping right next to the boat. Ron had one ram the side of his boat yesterday. He is certain that the fish still has a headache.

Eight miles before the finish line, a call is made to Andy's friend, Niccole, to make sure she's en route to Winona with Ron's van. She's on her way, and will be standing by for the next call with more specific directions.

It is 3:00 as we approach Lock & Dam No. 5A, on the north side of Winona. The plan is to lock through, paddle another thirty minutes and exit at the downtown landing. Andy makes contact with the lockmaster. Bad news, a northbound barge is going to be given priority over the southbound kayaks. Not wanting to risk having Niccole wait, we decide to turn and paddle one mile upstream, then one mile west beyond a cluster of small islands and marshland to the spillway, where there are supposed to be two boat landings. The map lacks sufficient detail, but is clear enough to set a new waypoint. We should arrive ahead of Niccole, giving us time to change clothes and repack the boats for the trip home.

I am the first to reach the spillway with Andy close behind. We're surprised to find that the landing we have been honing in on for the past forty minutes turns out to be on the downstream side of a six to eight foot drop in the spillway. We will have to portage to get to it, and we don't like portages. After another quick review of the map, it is determined that the second landing is above the spillway, but is tucked in a bay a half-mile up the shore. The other three in the group are still paddling toward the spillway several hundred yards away as Andy and I turn upstream. I signal them with a wave of my paddle thinking this should be intuitive: "We are changing directions."

Joan, Ron, and Harvey continue on toward the spillway. I then signal with a small air horn. I watch as the three close the distance to the drop, and then finally turn upstream. I assume they saw, heard, and understood the signals but were simply going in closer to check it out.

When the three arrive at the landing, they tell Andy and me how dangerously close they came to going over the drop. It turns out they neither saw nor heard me signaling. Sitting low in their kayaks, it was impossible for them to see the actual change in river elevation. The spillway, which stretches seventy-five yards across the river has only three warning buoys; one on each end and one in the middle. There are no barriers or any warning signs with words of caution. They didn't realize the peril before them until they saw a pick-up truck disappear as it backed down the boat ramp on the downstream side with an empty trailer, and then reappear moments later loaded with a large fishing boat.

"You got to be careful if you don't know where you're going, because you might not get there." -Lawrence Peter "Yogi" Berra, major league baseball player (1925-)

It is only a few minute wait for Niccole before loading the gear for the trip home. Again, in an effort to protect the more sensitive audience, there will not be any discussion regarding the encounter between Ron's van and a wild turkey.

Trip Report
- 616.6 miles completed (26.7% of total trip)
- 1,690.4 to The Gulf

[Leg 9]

Winona, MN to Thompson, IL; 202.9 River Miles

Monday, September 4, 2006 – Labor Day

It's mid-afternoon when Luke connects with me at my house. Andy has spent the weekend in Minneapolis with his sister and will be picked up on the way through. Tony is busy at school getting smarter as each day goes by, and adds one more section of river to his list of make-up sessions. The starting point for this leg of the trip is in Winona, MN. It's a five hour drive, though we somehow manage to stretch it into seven before reaching Winona City Park at 10:00.

"Time is a dressmaker specializing in alterations." -Faith Baldwin, novelist (1893–1978)

Tuesday, September 5, 2006

After an early breakfast, it's straight to Weenonah Canoe/Current Designs Kayak, whose headquarters are located here in Winona. Andy met the marketing manager, Bill, on the river during the last trip. Bill said for the paddlers to be sure to stop by when we get to Winona. We do as we are told, but Bill is out of town. The receptionist calls the CEO, Mike Cichanowski, (pronounced the same as it is spelled). Mike is Bill's father-in-law and is anxious to hear about the trip. His first question though is, "Do you have any gear in need of repair?" Andy told him of the rudder problems on his Current Designs

Storm due to his crash on the rocks. Ten minutes later, Andy's boat is inside the shop being taken care of.

After an extensive tour of the factory and learning everything anyone ever wanted to know about the making of kayaks, Luke asks about direct sales. "Not a problem." The bargains are too good to pass up. Before leaving, I pick up a new paddle, Luke buys a new boat and paddle, and Andy gets off easy, walking away with a free baseball cap and a brand new rudder assembly at no charge.

Though one of the rules in the club is, "You can't have too many kayaks," this isn't the case when you're on a paddling trip a few hundred miles away from home. Luke's old boat is left behind at the warehouse. We will pick it up on the way back home at the end of the week. Mike suggests parking Luke's truck & trailer at his "river house" because it would be safer there than anywhere else. The river house is eight river miles downstream from the intended launch site. We decide to sacrifice the lost miles in lieu of a safer environment.

The kayak factory tour, visiting, and shopping has caused a much later start than desired. It's not until 2:00 when we arrive at Mike's river house. The place is absolutely beautiful! If this is his second home, his primary residence must be really extraordinary. Thirty minutes of hauling gear down to the river, and the kayaks are finally water ready.

"Rivers know this: there is no hurry. We shall get there some day." -A. A. Milne, Pooh's Little Instruction Book

A couple hours from leaving Winona, we enter Lake Onalaska behind Lock and Dam No. 7, near LaCrosse, WI where the

river is nearly four miles wide. Over millions of years, inland seas across North America advanced and retreated several times, leaving sediments that became the dolomite, shale and sandstone that eventually formed the river bluffs in this area. About a hundred million years ago, the land in the midcontinent began to be uplifted. Water began to cut valleys through the uplifted plain. When the last glacier retreated about ten thousand years ago, Lake Agassiz was formed in northern Minnesota, eastern North Dakota and southern Canada. It drained through the present Minnesota River valley carving the river valley considerably deeper than it is now. As the volume decreased, the river dropped sediment, leaving fill as much as two hundred feet deep. Subsequent wind and water erosion sliced out terraces of the deposited material within the valley, creating a home for two hundred eighty-five species of birds and over fifty species of mammals. Most common to the area are the beaver, muskrat, deer, raccoon, red and gray fox, cottontail rabbit, gray and fox squirrel, thirteen-lined ground squirrel, chipmunk, striped skunk and several species of moles, shrews and mice. There are also twenty-three species of reptiles and thirteen species of amphibians. This area is also rich in fresh water mussels. There are more species of mussels in the Mississippi river watershed than in any other in the United States. [4]

"Now the Lord God had formed out of the ground all the beasts of the field and all the birds of the air. He brought them to the man to see what he would name them; and whatever the man called each living creature, that was its name."
-Genesis 2:19, The Message

The plan is to paddle as many miles as possible between now and next Sunday, hopefully ending up close to Davenport, IA, two hundred fifty miles down river. We will rent a U-Haul truck to get us and our equipment back upriver to Winona.

A 3–5 mph tailwind allows Luke and me a chance to try out our new sails. They work great, as does my marine radio and the other new equipment worth mentioning, i.e., porta-johns for personal use inside the kayaks, eliminating the need to find convenient stopping spots along the river.

Two locks and six hours after our start, Brownsville, MN is the chosen stopover for the night. There's a campground on river-right where we find the office closed and no signs forbidding tent camping. Fair enough, we'll find a level spot down by the river and settle up with the manager in the morning.

A pickup truck arrives when we are about 80% complete in getting our temporary accommodations ready for inhabitants. We pause to see if Pickup Guy has any objections to camping here. Waiting… Waiting… He eventually stops staring from inside the cab, gets out and walks away in the opposite direction. It looks like a definite green light. After the tents are completely erected, Pickup Guy and (most likely) his girl-friend, emerge surreptitiously from the shadows like a couple of feral cats set on protecting their territory. He's a little more round than tall, with a full face of grey stubble, and is wearing a pair of washed-out Oshkosh bibs, a red plaid flannel shirt, and a bright yellow and white baseball cap. The girlfriend… well… it's probably been at least forty years since she looked her absolute best.

"You can't pitch no tents hea' (pronounced hee'-ah)!"

In unison, "What!?!?"

Obviously, the man is caught off guard, and for the lack of anything else to say, he repeats his first statement.

Andy, "Okay. Where can we put up our tents?"

Pointing across the park toward the tree line, "Over thar, past the fence."

"Sounds good. We'll move."

"You can't do that. You gotta buy a camp pass."

"Where do we do that?"

"Right thar at the office."

"The office is closed."

"That's right. The park is closed! It closed at 10:00. How'd you guys get hea?"

"We came down the river. We're paddling kayaks and need a place to camp. I looked around for signs and didn't see anything indicating that tent camping is not allowed. Can we pay in the morning, or pay you now?"

"Ya. You can pay me. It's $17.00 per tent."

"$17.00!!! You're crooks."

"We're not crooks. The camp belongs to the county. It's thar rules. We just like to hep out."

"We'll be leaving."

"All crime is a kind of disease and should be treated as such." -Mahatma Gandhi (1869–1948)

Everything is taken down and repacked in the boats. I check my GPS and find I have marked three more campsites within the next two miles. We paddle to each site. Either the map used to mark the waypoints was incorrect or the campsites are no longer being maintained. Anyway, we can't find them. We continue to paddle downstream searching the shoreline for any place that we think will work.

At midnight, we spot a light affixed high on a pole a few hundred yards back in a bay. From the channel, two or maybe three cars can be seen parked in the opening. Paddling across two acres of pungent smelling algae to investigate, we cautiously approach the shoreline as the full moon, together with the mercury vapor security light muster a range of long muddled shadows stretching out across the property and onto the water. The old cars are nested in grass up to their headlights, poised and ready for the junk yard. Rotting planks precariously balanced on rocks and stumps along the shore simulate docks that lead out to three rather large homemade houseboats which are more or less floating on a cluster of fifty-five gallon drums; many of which appear to be close to liberation by unseen forces from below. Each of these not-so-seaworthy vessels has a large wrap-around deck, long past due for any rudimentary TLC. The scene conjures up flashbacks from the movie *Deliverance.* Without any discussion, we normally brazen explorers leave in silence.

An hour later, Andy's flashlight finds an old reflective sign along the shore recommending a stop at the Shellhorn Bar & Grill. The beach is narrow but it's the best option yet.

(Just wide enough)

"Ka-Ka-Ska-Ska"

A trail snakes through the underbrush and up across the nearby railroad tracks leading to the drinking establishment on the other side of the highway. Andy goes over to check if it is okay to camp at the landing. The young lady replies, "Yes. Make yourselves at home. There should be a fire ring there too if you need it." Now that's more like it.

"Kindness is in our power, even when fondness is not."
-Samuel Johnson, lexicographer (1709–1784)

Bedtime is 2:00 A.M. after logging in a respectable thirty-six miles.

Wednesday, September 6, 2006

Reluctantly, we arise at 8:00am. Breakfast varies from peanut butter and jelly on a bagel to tuna on a cracker. PowerAde pulls double duty as both juice and coffee.

The morning paddle is basically uneventful, stopping for an hour over noon at the London Bistro in Genoa, WI. Throughout the afternoon, everyone is off doing their own thing, displaced over thousands of yards of open water, paddling along in silence, enjoying the river at its best. No one looks back at what is behind, only ahead to what awaits. Along the way are hundreds of pelicans, geese, and numerous eagles and egrets. Large fish are plentiful too. Some that are jumping out of the water range three to four feet long – most likely carp. Our paddles often times bump into fish below and on occasion, fish ram the boats with quite a jolt. At one point, small bait fish practice a synchronized swimming routine while jumping in and out of my hand, as I rest it flat on the water's surfatce.

Jim Lewis

"Rivers and the inhabitants of the watery elements are made for wise people to contemplate and for fools to pass without consideration." -Izaak Walton

It's at Lansing, IA where we gather together for a snack and drift under the bridge and on through town. The intent is to get through Lock & Dam No. 9 and camp a mile beyond, at a wayside rest.

This time the campsite is exactly where it is supposed to be. We arrive at 10:30, satisfied with having conquered thirty-eight miles today. Soon after getting on shore, Chris France, a lady who lives a short distance away, shows up with four dogs; one border collie, one rottweiler, and two others who simply enjoy barking and jumping. It is deduced that this has to be a safe place if a lady can come down here "all alone" late at night.

Thursday, September 7, 2006

At 8:45, a barge that has been parked off the other shore overnight starts down river at the same time we do. The kayaks are kept at a steady rate of 5.2 mph alongside the barge and its eighteen containers for the next nine miles before the *Crimson Pride* pulls over. We continue on, certain the barge crew is exhausted from the pace and can no longer keep up.

Lunch is at the Marquette Café & Bar shortly before noon and the waitress wants to know the story. After hearing the Reader's Digest version of the trip down from the Headwaters, her only response is, "You guys are crazy!"

The comment stirs a recollection to yesterday when, soon after having gotten underway, a lady from a passing pontoon boat shouted, "Wow! You guys are brave!"

"What could they possibly know that we don't?"

"Ka-Ka-Ska-Ska"

"Some people are brave; others are just too stupid to be afraid." -Philip R. Breeze, author

Not quite three hours later, it's a stop in Clayton, IA for an hour at Bill's Boat Landing for refreshments.

The next stop, and the last for the day, is at 8:50, almost an hour past sunset in Cassville, WI. We've logged in a total of forty miles since breakfast. According to my GPS, the way-point set for this campground is another two tenths of a mile down river. However, it looks like a city park on river-left. Even more enticing is a small cinder block building with a sign, "Public Toilets & Showers". This is too good to be true! We pull the boats up on shore to check it out. We find a much smaller notice; "No Camping" encrypted below the larger letters that were visible from the river. "Well, this calls for nothing more than simply being discreet." Luke sets up behind the bathhouse next to a Coke machine. The Coke machine is much too noisy for me, so I take cover by the pavilion. Andy pitches his tent in the shadows beneath the oak trees not too far away. Camp is set up, showers taken, and it's off to forage for food.

Two blocks beyond the railroad crossing adjacent to the park, and west three more blocks, we enter the only open business along the street. Beer happens to be the most popular entrée. We go for the burgers. While sitting here, it's difficult to ignore how the building shakes vigorously every thirty to forty minutes. It is truly a strange phenomenon.

We're back at the city park/campsite at little past 10:00, as a train races through the crossing toward some unknown eastern destination. At the same time, another passes going west on a second set of tracks. (Somewhere, a sixth grader is struggling with his homework assignment to find the exact time these two trains, going in opposite directions, would meet. It's right now!) Evidently there is no speed limit through town because the trains do not even make an attempt to slow down. Now imagine the sound of the two heavily loaded freight trains doing at least 50 mph clambering over the loose timbers supporting the tracks at the crossing, combined with the DING, DING, DING of the warning bell, and you got yourself a chaotic combination of rumbling clatter that would drown out the screeching of a dozen cheetahs celebrating the capture of a gazelle, to say nothing of an old Coke machine that I thought earlier was too loud. Andy wants to know if anyone wants to purchase a set of ear plugs for $10.00. There are no takers.

"Every increased possession loads us with new weariness." -John Ruskin, author, art critic, and social reformer (1819–1900)

Luke and I are confident the trains will soon be resting for the night. Wrong. The trains continue to pass through every hour, and more than once, the two-train thing is replicated. The trains do not rest, nor do Luke and I.

Friday, September 8, 2006

Standing outside my tent at 7:00, Andy says in a stage whisper, "Jim, it's time to get up. I think there's a family reunion setting up about twenty-six yards from your tent."

I am out of my tent in less than five minutes. Our vagabond camp comes down a lot faster than it had gone up the night before. While Luke and I are finishing getting ready for the day, Andy strolls over to the gathering of the locals. There is no family reunion. It's a Farmer's Market. Andy walks past a lady with a large life-like chicken on her head. "I like your hat!"

"Thanks. It clucks."

Andy, pointing to the hat, "Make it happen." Lady does, and Andy's day is off to a good start.

With no residual sign of any drifters having camped in the city park, we leave again for downtown. More places are open, and the one that attracts us this morning is the River's Café. There we meet Lonnie Henderson, a local who has a small wood working shop down the street. He makes tourist stuff like boxes, baskets, and shelves.

Andy listens intently to Lonnie, but Luke and I are distracted by what is taking place at the counter. Another local, who Lonnie has introduced as a cousin of the guy who makes chainsaw furniture, is critiquing Waitress Catie's attire. He wants to know why she is wearing the same shirt she had worn the day before. Catie claims she had retrieved it from the clean clothes basket. When questioned further, however, she couldn't actually recall having laundered the shirt. The cousin of the chainsaw craftsman says, "The only surefire way to determine if laundry is clean is ..." then demonstrates – by lifting his arm and smelling to check for freshness.

"The end of the human race will be that it will eventually die of civilization." -Ralph Waldo Emerson, writer and philosopher (1803–1882)

After finishing our eggs and hash browns, Andy tags along with Lonnie to check out his workshop. Luke and I head off to the grocery store.

Twenty minutes later and together again, it's time to return to the park. As we approach the railroad crossing, a police car is across the street to our right. It is parked facing the opposite direction, up tight next to the bright red Park & Grounds dump truck. The assumption is that the lawman and the city employee are talking about us. The clue: Park & Grounds Guy is pointing at us. We turn left and keep walking, avoiding any eye contact.

Sure enough, the cop does a u-turn and pulls up along side. "Were you guys camped in the park last night?"

"Yes sir," looking down at the ground like small children awaiting their punishment.

"Not a problem. It's just that we've gotten quite a few calls about your tents in the park. I tried to find you last night to tell you to be sure to be out of there at sun up. But I couldn't catch up to you."

I'm impressed. "You worked last night and again this morning?"

"Yep…one man show. I got a call from the mayor too."

"Wow! The entire police force was looking for us last night. And this morning, we're the highest priority on the mayor's agenda."

I apologize for the trouble caused.

"Don't worry about it and have a good day."

We thank him for his kindness. Shaking its dust from our feet, we bid the town farewell.

It's twenty-seven miles to the city of Dubuque with the first fifteen miles accomplished using nothing but wind power. When the river turns towards the east/southeast, we are faced with a stiff headwind for the next twelve miles. Waves break over the front of the boats, all the way up to the deck bags. The headwind finally subsides when we enter the city.

"Ka-Ka-Ska-Ska"

It could be a special occasion or a daily event, we're not sure, but there are two 'dragon boats' on the river. Each one is crewed by two screamers giving direction to the twenty paddlers on board. As I approach the first of the big boats, I give in to the urge, and challenge them to a race to the bridge a hundred yards out. In one person's mind it looks like a photo-finish; to others, it's more obvious that the old guy just comes in a close second.

"It is not how old you are, but how you are old." -Jules Renard, writer (1864–1910)

Lunch is at the Ice Harbor Galley. The chef feels bad that the server neglected to announce today's special (deep-fried cod fish). He brings out a complimentary order for each of us, in addition to the meal already ordered. This means we'll be working extra hard this afternoon to get rid of the extra calories.

The remainder of the afternoon passes without any noteworthy events. Then, about an hour before sunset, I flag down a personal water craft to see if the small channel on river-right could perhaps be a shortcut to the main channel. Once assured that it reconnects downstream, I ask if the couple has any ice. They do, and also offer up champagne.

Of course, you can't let that pass without questioning why they would have it onboard. The young lady on the back explains that they had been on a picnic on the island. She holds up her left hand to display a new ring, "We just got engaged!" We're the first told. Congrats to Annette Rife and Clete Brehm.

The ice from Annette and Clete isn't going to last long, so when we encounter two boats anchored in the channel a mile downstream, three guys and four women, we hit them up for more ice. It has been a long hot afternoon, and there are several hours of paddling to go. The folks on the pleasure crafts are willing to share more than their ice. One of the guys asks us if we want to buy their women. Negotiations end as quickly as they began when one of the other boaters proposes, "How about if we give you our women, and you give us back the ice?"

A quick vote is taken. "We'll just keep the ice. Thanks."

"A man has to live with himself, and he should see to it that he always has good company." - **Charles Evans Hughes, jurist (1862–1948)**

The next lock is fifteen miles ahead, but we are determined to find a campsite located on the upstream side. We cut through backwaters to the far shore two miles above the lock where there is supposed to be a designated campground. It's incredibly surreal. Fish of all sizes ram into the boats and jump like popcorn as the kayaks navigate through giant Alice-in-Wonderland-like lily pads suspended well over two feet above the water supported on half-inch diameter stems. When hit with the paddle, they bend down to give us a pat on the head for a job well done. This is all in the brilliant light of the full moon. It's an experience that's hard to beat.

The search for a campsite on this side of the lock is unsuccessful. We lock through to continue the quest downstream. The GPS indicates the location of a cemetery not much more than two miles downstream of the lock. I am positive dry and level ground can be found there. Andy and Luke do not think camping in a cemetery is something they would like to do.

They do agree, however, to go there to check it out. As we get close, a beach is discovered directly across the bay from the cemetery. It's a beach that is neither dry nor level. As a matter of fact, it's a muddy incline, but it will have to do because Luke and Andy refuse to take advantage of the other opportunity. We've covered fifty-two miles and at 12:30 A.M., we're not going to continue the search for anything better.

Saturday, September 9, 2006

We're up at 7:30 and on the water one hour later without taking time for breakfast. Luke tells us that he had been really hungry when he crawled into his sleeping bag the night before so he got out a package of beef jerky. He remembers taking one bite. He awoke this morning to find that he had never even finished chewing it.

"There is no pillow so soft as a clear conscience." -French proverb

Strong head winds are the theme during the first fifteen miles. Making progress is slower than it has been, but we're still able to pump out 4 mph. We make seventeen miles before stopping for lunch in Savanna, IL.

In between trips to the buffet at Happy Joe's Pizza, phone calls are made to try to arrange for the U-Haul truck needed for tomorrow's return trip back upriver. The places called have either closed for the day or have caller ID. Car rentals and other truck rentals are checked out. They are equally futile. Luke suggests going to the auto parts store down the street. "We get all the pieces-parts they have in stock for a 1974 AMC Gremlin, and make our own car to transport our crap upriver."

Andy and I are about to buy into the idea when the waiter, who has been listening in on our quandary, tells us about a

U-Haul truck rental in Thompson, IL, only thirteen miles down river. The truck rental is run by a motel and should be open. He helps find the phone number and "Bingo!" Two trucks are scheduled to be back on the lot at 5:00. The new plan: Paddle to Thompson and call it a trip. We'll get home early Sunday morning.

As we approach Thompson, I stop to chat with two fishermen who are standing in a bass boat near a bay filled with the same giant lily pads encountered the night before.

"Excuse me. Is there a special name for this foliage?"

"What?"

"Is there a special name for this foliage?"

With a look blending disbelief and distrust, the reply comes slowly from the big guy standing in the rear of the boat, "Lily pads."

"Wow. Where we come from, lily pads are only about six to eight inches in diameter and lay flat on the water."

"Where do you come from?"

"Northern Minnesota."

Looking down at me, studying my kayak from one end to the other, "You bring that thing all the way from Minnesota?"

"Yep."

"You're not right!" That's it. That's all he says, as he turns away and focuses once more on his fishing. (This ends our brief, but quality time together.)

"Criticism, like rain, should be gentle enough to nourish a man's growth without destroying his roots." -Frank A. Clark, writer (1911–)

We continue a mile beyond Thompson in search of a way to get off the river that is hopefully close to the U-Haul location. I have it marked on my GPS based on the waiter's information. The acceptable landing we find is on private land, but that's okay. No one is home. The three of us exit the Mississippi leaving all the gear behind. We hike down a dirt road, through the woods, and across a corn field. After that, it's another half-mile or so walking along the narrow shoulder of a paved county road to the "X" that marks the spot. There, at the coordinates where the motel and U-Haul is supposed to be, we find the Illinois State Prison. (Perhaps, the waiter was trying to tell us something.)

Luke makes another call to the U-Haul place. This time, a grumpy guy answers instead of the helpful young lady who he had talked with earlier. Grumpy Guy is definitely not a happy camper. He does not care that we are lost and on foot, and insists that he does not know anything about us needing a truck. Luke convinces him that we were told by his coworker that a truck is available, and that if he could provide direction, we'll be there shortly. The correct location is another mile to the east. It's a nice day for a walk. Besides, there is no offer to come pick us up.

The place is pretty nice. It's out in the middle of nowhere, yet looks relatively new and well maintained. There is also a restaurant located directly off the motel lobby. "Let's plan on getting something to eat here before leaving."

Immediately upon entering, Luke and Andy duck off to a small sitting area adjacent to the front desk and out of sight. Grumpy Guy is behind the counter wearing a brown felt beret on top his obviously bald head, and a label on his pale yellow shirt boasting of his position of assistant manager. He is still not happy. If anything, he's worse now than when Luke had talked with him twenty minutes ago. I swing into action using all the teachings of Dale Carnegie. Soon, there is slight evidence that the grumpiness is being diluted, but the stench of bad attitude still lingers in the air. As we get to the part of the rental process that requires checking the vehicle's fuel level and mileage, Grumpy Guy says, "I don't even know if the tank is full or what the odometer reading is. Now I have to leave things here unattended to go get that stuff!"

I am quick to volunteer to run out and retrieve the information from the truck parked on the far end of the lot.

Grumpy Guy tosses the keys across the counter. "Here. Bring it up and park it right out front."

I snatch the keys and promptly exit, glad to get away for a few minutes. I get the truck and do exactly as told, so as not to further upset Grumpy Guy. PROBLEM – "...right out front." is a vestibule designed to allow passage to vehicles needing no more than 11'3" of clearance. Unfortunately, the truck I am driving requires a clearance of 11'6"... KABOOM! (Probably an understatement.)

Inside, Andy and Luke being their usual incredibly perceptive selves, coupled with having been around me for some time, have an immediate and full understanding of what has just taken place. Grumpy Guy seems to have an instant grasp on the situation as well and begins to shout a few (no, a lot of) words not normally considered acceptable in public. He, along with Andy and Luke, cannot get out of the building fast enough.

Outside, Grumpy Guy enters into a deep state of denial. "It can't be. It can't be. No one can be that stupid!"

His tirade continues on for a few minutes accompanied with occasional kicks at the ground, head shaking and flailing of arms as if being attacked by a swarm of bees. Then, the outburst subsides, just a touch, and Grumpy Guy retreats back into the motel muttering (no, still shouting) more words of discontent.

Meanwhile, the three amigos, who are left outside are wondering, *"What are the chances of finding another U-Haul center within walking distance?"* The blood running from my mouth as a result of having been ~~bumped~~ (no, smashed) on the steering wheel when the truck came to an abrupt stop does not seem to be a primary concern of anyone. Focus is instead shifted to assessing the damage of the vehicle and the structure. The truck has one broken clearance light, and only a minor dent on the overhang above the cab. It's about three inches deep and measures six to eight inches across. The building on the other hand appears to have suffered a smidgen more harm. A four foot section of the fascia material near the point of impact is currently holding its own in the battle against gravity, but it is not known for how long. It is also noted that the columns supporting the outboard side of the vestibule are now leaning like a tree that has long since given in to prevailing winds. Further study reveals that the structure has shifted from where it had been attached to the main roof. Shingles in the valley where the vestibule is connected to the roof are pulled apart on the side where the impact occurred, and are all bunched up on the opposite side.

"When you think of the long and gloomy history of man, you will find more hideous crimes have been committed in the name of obedience than have ever been committed in the name of rebellion." -C.P. Snow, scientist and writer (1905–1980)

The three outside continue to discuss the situation at great depth and finally come to a unanimous acceptance of the hypothesis. "The truck collided with the vestibule because of simple physics and a simple operator. The dent and the broken clearance light may or may not have occurred at the time of impact. No preoperational inspection of the vehicle's condition had been performed. Likewise, the integrity of the fasteners used to secure the fascia was not noted at the time of our arrival. Therefore, the material may have been dangling as it currently is for who knows how long. The remaining findings are attributed to sloppy craftsmanship during construction." (In no way should this theory be construed as a means to transfer responsibility or blame.)

"We lie the loudest when we lie to ourselves." -Eric Hoffer, philosopher and author (1902–1983)

Okay, now that we know what could have happened, we are ready for the police or whatever comes next. I am urged to go in and find out what Grumpy Guy is up to. However, before I have time to get to the door, Grumpy Guy appears and orders me inside. Inside, I am given the rental contract and a vehicle inspection form noting the dent. A comment is written on the inspection form indicating the extent of the truck's damage and that it occurred prior to the actual rental. I sign the papers and begin to apologize, but Grumpy Guy grabs the copies he needs, hands me my copies and says, "Get out of here!"

Finding out that we still have the rental truck, Andy and Luke do their impersonation of Grumpy Guy in denial, "It can't be. It can't be. No one can be that stupid!"

It is decided that we should probably be on our way and find someplace else to eat. Luke and Andy insist I drive, probably because I have the most experience with the truck.

Back at the riverside, we load up and point towards home. En route, Luke calls Mike in Winona to ask if it's okay to get the pickup and trailer from the river house and the kayak from the warehouse. It's not a problem. Mike will make sure the boat at the warehouse will be outside.

At 1:20 A.M., I turn the U-Haul down the private drive to Mike's house. Luke hops out to get his truck and says he will follow us downtown. As we turn back onto the four-lane from Mike's, Andy sees a sheriff's patrol car going in the opposite direction and says, "You might as well pull over." As the U-Haul slows onto the shoulder, the squad car is bouncing across the grassy median with the red lights flashing. Luke doesn't even wave as he drives right on by.

"Do you know why I stopped you?"

"Yes, because we're coming out of **Mike's** private drive with a U-Haul filled with kayaks."

"What were you doing there?"

"**Mike** was kind enough to allow us to ..."

After I drop **Mike's** name a few more times, the deputy does a radio check on my driver's license and returns. He wants to hear more about the trip before wishing us well. I'm at least smart enough to tell the deputy we are on our way to Mike's warehouse to get the other boat, most likely saving another run- in with The Man.

At the warehouse, we transfer the gear from the U-Haul to the trailer and then drop the rental truck off downtown. We arrive at Andy's sister's apartment building at 4:00, Sunday morning. She does not respond to a phone call and though Andy does not have keys to her place nor his car, he is sure that he will be able to locate her soon. He says it is okay for Luke and me to go on.

Luke has been driving since Winona and now passes his pickup keys to me, so I can drive the remaining four hours to Grand Rapids. The last words from Luke before he falls asleep are, "Try not to hit anything." We're home at 8:30 A.M., declaring an end to our reign of terror.

"True remorse is never just a regret over consequences; it is a regret over motive." -Mignon McLaughlin, author (1915–)

Trip Report
- 819.5 miles completed (35.5% of total trip)
- 1,487.5 to New Orleans

[2007]

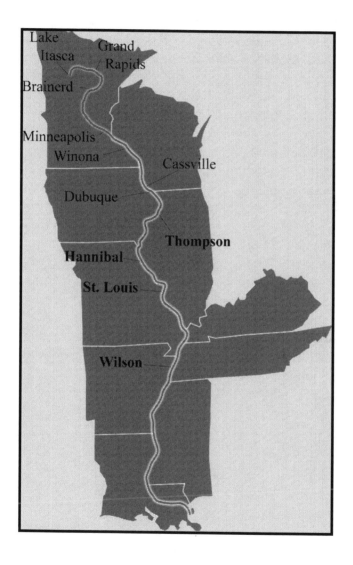

2007 Introduction

Once again, winter found the crazies out in their kayaks every Saturday always trying to beat the extremes, regardless of the weather. No matter how far the mercury dropped, the water was open at the Minnesota Power Landing. On February 3, 2007, five Itasca Kayakers, being cautious to keep any exposed skin to a minimum, hit the water in an unbelievable -22 F and a wind chill close to -50 F. The five included: Harvey Frisco, Joan Bibeau, Ron Ulseth I, Ed Murray, and me. It was one of those days when your mom would tell you to dress in layers and keep them all on.

When the wind chill makes the temperature feel like -28 F, exposed skin can freeze in under thirty minutes. When it drops to -40 F, frostbite can occur in less than ten minutes. Take the wind chill down to -55 F, and you're in danger within two minutes. Anything colder than that and Environment Canada warns, you shouldn't go outside at all.[5] It's a good thing Canada is a hundred miles to the north! In spite of the risks involved, the outing made for some great photo opportunities as God's creation was presented at its best. Canada Geese stood on the ice watching in disbelief the kayaks paddle by a few feet away in the dense vapor rising from the frigid water.

"Ka-Ka-Ska-Ska"

(Heading out at a -22 F)

For what it's worth, I received a call in late January, 2007 from the insurance company handling the U-Haul claim for the damages to the truck and the building in the September 9 incident. The claim was in its final stages and the only thing missing in the file was my version of the event. I told the insurance adjuster the 'truth as I knew it.' After reviewing the facts with a supervisor, I was told there would not be any further follow up. I would not be responsible for any portion of the damages. The call came on the last day of my working career; starting retirement with a clean slate.

Another personal note... Tony's second priority in life has evidently changed from "Volleyball / Girls – in that order" to Girls / Volleyball. He and Chandra have started dating. Hang in there for the rest of the story.

On April 3, 2007, Grand Rapids received six inches of beautiful fresh fallen snow while the wind blew at a not so attractive 20–30 mph. Over the next two days, the temperature hovered in the seasonal norms of twenties and low thirties. And though the weather to the south was not much different, it did not change our plans to leave for the next leg of the trip on Friday, April 6.

"Yesterday is but a dream,
　　and tomorrow only a vision.
But today, well lived will make every yesterday
　　a dream of happiness and every tomorrow
a vision of hope."
Sanskrit Proverb

[Leg 10]

Thompson IL, to St. Louis, MO;
352.6 River Miles

Friday, April 6, 2007

As scheduled, Luke, Andy, and I depart from Grand Rapids at noon and meet Tony in Moose Lake, MN ninety miles down the street. Another ten hours and a couple of brief stops later, we arrive at the Super 8 in Clinton, IA, our "campground" for the first night out.

We arise at 6:40 A.M. for an early start, though nearly two hours pass by the time the river is in sight. After getting ready, it's a stop at McDonald's for breakfast, and then we take one of my shortcuts. We drive through every backstreet, alley, and narrow county road to travel the six miles to Lock & Dam No. 13. This is about eight river miles south of last fall's take-out in Thompson, IL. Again, we are opting for the better parking spot in lieu of river miles. Luke's truck will be left here on government land until Thursday, when a friend, Mark Scotch, from Wisconsin will swing by to get it. Mark will drive it south and connect with us downstream, leaving his car here until the return trip next weekend.

At 9:45, the boats are packed, the truck is secure, and the kayaks push off into the flooded wooded area below the lock. The temperature has not risen from an overnight low of 19 F and a check with the anemometer shows nothing less than a 20 mph northwest wind with plenty of gusts just short of 30 mph.

❖ ❖ ❖

The following seven-plus hours are spent battling wind and waves, while we are dampened by an occasional shower. There is no time to stop to take photos of the ice figurines formed on the gear lashed to the deck, or the eagles perched along the river, or the hundreds of pelicans, or the large flocks of annoying cormorants preying on innocent fish, or even the great blue heron seen standing on a dock trying to down its fresh catch while the kayaks slice through the choppy water a few feet away.

We reach the Lindsay Park Yacht Club in Davenport, IA, at 5:00 in the afternoon. All slips are empty and the place appears to be deserted. It is too inviting to pass up, considering everyone is cold, wet and tired. Simply put, it's not been pleasant. This is as good a place as any to call it a day, after a challenging thirty-eight miles.

"No sensible decision can be made any longer without taking into account not only the world as it is, but the world as it will be." -Isaac Asimov, scientist and writer (1920–1992)

It's apparent the slips were not designed for kayakers. The decking of the docks is situated over three feet above the waterline. It is a struggle to get the gear, the boats, and ourselves, lifted out of the water to safety. Once done, I walk up the ramp towards the clubhouse to see if there's a way through, or over, the perimeter fence. Much to my surprise, there are lights on inside the clubhouse which were not obvious from down by the river because of the heavily tinted windows overlooking the marina. Even more of a surprise is, it looks like there are people inside. I try the door and walk in. An older gentleman sitting at the bar greets me. He says that they have been watching, and were betting that at least one of us was saying, "Why didn't we start a motorcycle club?"

"Ka-Ka-Ska-Ska"

Frank, my new friend, introduces his daughter, Denise, son-in-law, Bruce, and a few of the other patrons to me as the other paddlers close in from behind. Only a few minutes into the conversation, but long enough to get an extremely condensed version of the adventure, Denise asks about our plans for tonight's lodging.

"We hoped to find a campground or motel close by."

"Do you want a free room for the night?"

I call for a quick vote. The decision is unanimous. It doesn't take an economics major to calculate that a free room is a better deal than having to pay for one.

Denise explains that she had recently won a night's lodging at the riverboat casino, moored two or three miles back upriver. She is willing to make a phone call to arrange for us to capitalize on her good fortune, as well as provide a ride. We order a couple rounds of Peppermint Pattys to warm us up, while details are worked out. Meanwhile, Frank tells Andy that he has always tried to be hospitable and kind to strangers, and has tried to raise his children with the same values.

"You can't live a perfect day without doing something for someone who will never be able to repay you." -John Wooden, sports coach (1910–)

Things are looking up, except for the injury sustained by Tony while getting his boat out of the water. A rather large sliver of wood punctured the palm of his right hand. It refused to be pulled free without leaving a good portion broken off well below the skin. A band-aid and a bit of antiseptic ointment will have to do for now. Andy cautions Tony that if he gets lockjaw, he will be left behind. It's the rule.

The room at the casino with two king size beds and a beautiful view overlooking the river is quickly transformed into a scene of a cheap laundry with wet clothes hanging from curtain rods, door hinges, lamps, and even the ceiling fan. After settling in, hot showers are next; then it's off to try to beat the house at the buffet.

It's the only gambling we do, and when done, we are positive the value of the food consumed is much greater than the $11.95 cost.

Sunday, April 8, 2007

The rain and snow in Grand Rapids and across the northland two weeks ago are now having a positive influence on the river level, (one foot below flood stage). According to the forecast, we will be riding this 'bump' with the advantage of the current running close to 4.5 mph for the remainder of the week. Hopefully, this will offset today's predicted headwinds of 15–25 mph.

Though we wake and greet the day at 6:30, catch the casino shuttle and consume a hurried breakfast at the gas station next to the yacht club, we do not make any headway down the river until four hours later. The plan for another early start was greatly hindered by a northbound barge arriving at Lock & Dam No.15 minutes ahead of the kayakers.

It's another day of enduring the elements and traveling through miles of undeveloped floodplain. By 4:00, everyone is again cold, wet, tired, hungry and in need of a stop. Muscatine, IA is the place. Muscatine began as a trading post founded in 1833 and was originally known as Casey's Woodpile; then was officially named Bloomington when incorporated in 1839. After realizing there were already too many Bloomingtons in the Midwest and mail delivery was becoming a problem, the city was renamed Muscatine. It is the only city in the United States with this name. A button company was founded here in 1884, producing buttons by punching them out of clam shells harvested from the river. Muscatine was known as the "Pearl Button Capital of the World." Hole-punched clam shells can still be found along the riverfront. [6] (Two months after we were here, much of this river town was either destroyed or heavily damaged when it was struck by an EF3 tornado on the afternoon of June 1, 2007.)

The boats are tied up at the city dock and we walk up to the Wood Fire Grill for a late lunch. Choices, choices and more choices; "Do we order coffee to warm up our insides or do we have a beer in hopes that it will help us to forget how cold we are?" It's two for two.

When our salads arrive, Andy wants to know, "How is it that a person can paddle as hard as we have for hours on end, then sit down with a dinner fork and have hardly enough strength to pick up a tiny crouton?"

"Never eat more than you can lift." -Miss Piggy, a character in the cartoon The Muppet Show

We paddle until at least 9:00 before beginning to look for a campsite. By 10:00, we all are wishing the search would have started much earlier while there was still some daylight. The river current is much faster now, pushing toward 7 mph for this section. The result of the higher and faster water is a lot of floating debris, including large logs, creating a dreadfully unsafe condition – especially after dark. Searching his GPS, Andy locates an old road on the Illinois side of the river. He makes his way up on shore and discovers this is a peninsula with a somewhat level grassy clearing where the high-pressure gas line runs. It's not perfect, but it will do.

Fifty-four miles paddled today. Tonight's forecast is for clear skies and a low of 24 F.

Monday, April 9, 2007

The topic of conversation over breakfast this morning is all about the animal noises heard throughout the night. It seems we were infringing on the territory of resident beavers, coyotes, owls, and a number of other birds and a few animals not easily identified. As Tony is packing up, he asks if someone can recognize what it is that is lying on the ground beneath where I had my sleeping bag. "It is either a very poor specimen of animal feces or something that has been dead for quite a few days."

Luke, evidently an expert on such things, says he'll check it out as soon as he is finished with his oatmeal. The verdict is that the unknown mass was at one time most likely a small bird of some sort. That's according to the expert, anyway.

"The pursuit of truth and beauty is a sphere of activity in which we are permitted to remain children all our lives."
-Albert Einstein, physicist, Nobel laureate (1879–1955)

Invigorated by the cold, we are able to get on the water by 8:00 and make good time against a merciless headwind. At the approach to Lock & Dam No.18 a few minutes before noon, I make contact with the lockmaster on the radio. There will be a minimum of ninety minutes delay – once more, due to northbound traffic. Not to be held hostage again, we turn about and paddle back upstream a few hundred yards to escape the draw of the dam. We then cross over to the west side of the river where it is flooded out well beyond the spillway. I go on ahead to explore this option. In doing so, I startle at least two hundred unsuspecting pelicans to flight. Though the thunderous flapping of their wings sounds like an auditorium filled with applause, I do not believe it is a sign of being welcomed.

The 'waterway' through the wooded area looks a bit hazardous, but most likely manageable. I edge forward with caution, however, soon find myself beyond the point of no return and overwhelmed by the torrent. The floodwater is not only rushing to get back to the main channel through a jumble of fallen trees along the river's edge, but with equal force is raging over a hillside down a ravine a hundred yards farther back in the trees. It is all I can do to control my boat, praying I can keep it straight and negotiate all the deadfall. The rudder cables are being put to the limits as I push the steering pedals with all I've got. By the time I reach the more stable flow out in front of the spillway, I am out of prayers and out of breath. My legs are literally shaking like a leaf, as I begin to relax. The others waiting above the spillway are unaware of what I just went through. Without hesitation, they accept my signal to come straight ahead over the drop of less than one foot. They all make it without incident.

"There's nothing more dangerous than a resourceful idiot." -Scott Adams, author and creator of Dilbert comic strip (1957–)

The wind tapers off through the afternoon, making the non-stop paddle to Fort Madison, IA a little more pleasurable. This area of the river is also known as Lake Cooper. With 30,000 acres of water, it is Iowa's largest lake. It's a good spot to have a late lunch at a diner a few blocks up from the public landing.

Afterward, as we are returning to the gear left by the river, a big fellow bundled up in a parka with a thick wool scarf wrapped around his neck three times is walking towards us. He stops directly in our path and asks, "Are you paddling down the river in those kayaks?"

It is affirmed. He shakes his head and begins to laugh. This is not a mere tee-hee type laugh, but one that can only come from deep down in the pit of the stomach – one that he had probably been holding inside for a long time – one that apparently wasn't easy to control, nor end. Not having a thorough understanding of what he finds so funny, nor interested in answering any more of his questions, we 'Hilarious Minnesotans' step around him and continue on their way.

It's nothing discussed, yet it's probably safe to say we all would feel better if people were to just tell us that they think we're crazy rather than laugh hysterically.

"Think not those faithful who praise all thy words and actions; but those who kindly reprove thy faults." -Socrates, philosopher (469?-399 BCE)

The sun sets quickly after we get underway. It brings to mind how difficult it was to find a campsite the night before. There is a small town, Montrose, IA, about ten miles downstream. That will be today's destination.

(Ten miles to go)

At Casey's Convenience Store, located two blocks from the river access, we are told there are no campgrounds or motels. It's 9:45. Clearly, options are quite limited. I ask the clerk if I could have the telephone number for the local police to see if we could get permission to camp in the gazebo at the park next to the river. (No need to have a repeat of the Cassville, WI incident.) The clerk hasn't got the number, but is able to provide contact information for the sheriff's office. I call, and am given the number for the police chief. Good. Progress is being made. It's hard to say how often over the years I have confused simple activity with actual progress, but within minutes, permission to lay claim to a homestead for the night in the park is granted.

"If anyone questions why you are there, just tell them I said it is okay." We have a roof over our heads and a safe place to sleep even though, the railroad tracks run less than thirty feet away.

No sooner do we get comfortable, but a visitor arrives. It is John Guyer, the chair of the city council. The police chief had called him. John wants to know if it would be alright to have someone from the newspaper come down in the morning to do a little story. "Of course. No problem." Ten minutes after John leaves, Roger and Mary Sue Chapfield from the newspaper show up. They do not want to risk missing this newsworthy event in the morning. Roger and Mary Sue hang around and visit until nearly midnight, sharing some interesting history about their community.

The city was originally named Mount of Roses and at one time the hillside along Bluff Park was covered in roses. Father Marquette and Louis Joliet, famous French explorers, stopped here to trade with the Indians and brought the message of Christianity. Montrose is also home to the first apple orchard in the state of Iowa, however, the orchard now sits beneath the waves of the Mississippi because it was submerged when the Keokuk Dam was built in 1912–13.

The park, where we kayakers have laid out our sleeping bags in the gazebo, was once the location of Fort Des Moines. Furthermore, during yesteryear, Montrose was home to an opera house, three general stores, a hardware store, drug store, garden tool factory, button factories and coal and lumber yards.

The historic Mormon Trail began here in the winter of 1847. The Mormons camped here for several days before beginning their westward trek. [7] (It is not known whether the Mormons had permission from the police chief – or, if the locals were as excited to see them as they are today's visitors.)

"Ka-Ka-Ska-Ska"

Tuesday, April 10, 2007

After breakfast at Casey's Convenience Store, Roger returns to take photos of our send-off. The wind is as strong today as it has been every day since starting this leg. Roger's parting words are, "At least you don't have any white caps today."

His words echo in my ears as I take the lead around the point of land protecting the river landing from the south. There the waves are between two and three feet, each with its very own little white cap.

The next hour and a half is spent taking the waves head on with the boats rising two feet or more on the crest, then slamming down again over and over. Finally, on the far side of the river and downstream about six miles, we group up for a break. From here we follow the shore line out of the wind.

Six more miles of paddling places us near Lock & Dam No. 19. The lock is on the opposite shore and the crossover feels incredibly dangerous. The wind is now pushing the white-capped waters at us from the side, while the current from the intense draw of the dam is pulling the kayaks into a pinch point between a southbound barge and the wall extending out from the lock. Each one of us makes it with room to spare but I, for one, am worn out by the time we reach safety.

I radio the lockmaster and am told the barge will take priority. Almost immediately the barge captain responds to the lockmaster, indicating that it would be okay for the kayaks to go in with them. They would watch out for the smaller crafts. Without hesitation or compassion, the lockmaster replies, "The kayaks can wait!" We wait almost two hours. It's cold sitting here that long, but the delay gives time for lunch and a much needed break.

The rest of the afternoon continues to be a battle against the headwind. It has increased to more than 30 mph, breaking the waves over the bow of the boats and spraying icy water in our faces with each stroke. (That's while trying to stay near shore, out of the brunt of the wind.)

"If you want total security, go to prison. There you're fed, clothed, given medical care and so on. The only thing lacking... is freedom." -Dwight D. Eisenhower, U.S. general and 34th president (1890–1969)

Canton, IA is where Gene Priede, who happens to be walking his dog down by the river, lends a helping hand when we arrive. Gene is excited to hear our story and doesn't give a second thought about offering a ride to the Canton Motel. It's 5:00. With only thirty-two miles behind us, our 'fun-meters' are pegged. We're calling it a day. Leaving the boats cabled together in the riverside park, we take with us what we need for the night.

Lyle, the owner of the motel, displays a first-class combination of pity and kindness by giving us a good rate for the night. During check-in, the small poodle with a four foot leash anchored to the leg of a couch six feet away is hard to ignore. From the time we stepped through the door, the little white curly-everywhere dog barked as it ran to the end of its tether and was recoiled back to the starting line before making the next lunge – again and again. As I sign the credit card statement, I tell Lyle, "I've got one at home just like that."

"Really? A toy poodle?"

"Nope. A short leash."

After a quick shower and a phone call to the local police asking them to keep an eye on the boats throughout the evening, it's a walk to the laundromat a block away. We need to wash the dirty stuff, and more importantly, to dry the wet stuff.

The laundromat is an excellent source of free entertainment for its patrons. There is not a machine in the place without some sort of message – either scrawled in magic marker, or as a hand written note affixed with tape cautioning people to check their pockets for everything from shotgun shells to live animals. Other memos include meticulous operating instructions informing the user of the correct method of placing coins in the slots and what steps are required to overcome each unique quirk. The only dryer that is apparently in working order has a 3X5 index card attached which reads:

1. Insert the coins in the slot.
2. Shut the door.
3. Look in the hole [an arrow drawn with magic marker connects the note to where a ¼" diameter hole has been drilled in the sheet metal face of the unit.]
4. Look up and back about 6–8".
5. You should see a flame.
6. If you do not see a flame, open the door and shut it.
7. Look in the hole again for the flame.
8. Repeat until you see a flame.

With the laundry done, the next stop is the Firehouse Bar for burgers, and a $5.00 bottomless glass of draft. By 10:00, it's back to the motel and prepare for bed. Tony is very concerned about the splinter still in his hand. It is not getting any better and is actually quite inflamed. Apparently tired of listening to my nonsense about red streaks, potential coma, and impending death, he makes a call to his cousin's wife, Erin, who is a nurse. Erin tells him that he should have it looked at sometime within the next day or so.

Wednesday, April 11, 2007

It has rained most of the night and continues to do so. Tony is the first to get out the door and returns after a quick trip to the gas station, "There is no point in going over there for anything to eat. I've purchased the last egg and sausage muffin."

While the others are rotating through the bathroom, Tony contacts a clinic about two miles away. "I'm going to walk over there and have someone check my hand and my infection." My twisted mind makes me question if these are two separate problems or one and the same. I don't get a response.

"No one would talk much in society, if he knew how often they were misunderstood by others." - Johann Wolfgang Von Goethe, writer (1749–1832)

Lyle had commented at the time of check-in that his dad runs a restaurant downtown called the Bird's Nest. Tony is told to meet us there when he is done at the clinic. Breakfast is an outstanding bargain: three pancakes, three eggs, three sausage patties, toast, and hash browns for $4.75. It sure beats a stupid egg and sausage muffin from the gas station.

Tony arrives after an hour or so. He was given a tetanus shot and claims he will live a long happy life. Back to the motel, check-out, and then hike to the boats. This is one more of those breathtaking 'Kodak Moments' not captured on film unless, of course, it was by someone driving along the street this morning. Whether photographed by passersby or not, the townsfolk are most likely still talking about the day they saw "four goofy-looking knuckleheads walking along the roadside in a steady rain, wearing life jackets and spray skirts, balancing kayak paddles on their shoulders...just walking along like they had no care in the world."

"Ka-Ka-Ska-Ska"

At the river, the boats are exactly where we left them, safe and sound. It is not certain whether or not this is a good thing. It would be pretty easy to abort the mission at this point if someone were to have taken them.

We finally push off ten minutes before noon with a target destination of Hannibal, MO, not quite thirty-four miles away.

"Do, or do not. There is no try." -Yoda, wise master of the Force, teacher of Jedi (1099–)

Though the wind isn't nearly as bad today, the rain continues for four of the long and tedious six hours of paddling to the goal. One highlight of the day is when Luke and Andy attempt sailing when the river, the wind, and the moons are all aligned. They hit a top speed of 9.5 mph. The downside is that they have to abort the effort after only two miles due to it being simply too cold to just sit in the cockpit holding onto the sail's guide ropes, not being able to paddle at the same time.

Another memorable time comes about midpoint in the trip at Lock & Dam No. 21 near Quincy, IL. The approach is again horribly difficult and treacherous – similar to that of Lock & Dam No. 19. It is déjà vu with the wind, the current, and the draw from the dam except this time, there is no barge in the picture. Again, we make it without incident and are relieved to have one more of these barriers behind us.

From Quincy, it is fifteen miles to Hannibal, best known as the boyhood home of author Samuel Clemons, aka Mark Twain, and the setting of his *The Adventures of Tom Sawyer* and *Adventures of Huckleberry Finn*.

As we reach Hannibal, I paddle close to shore near a restaurant where a couple of men are getting out of a car. I ask about a hotel in town and am told the Hotel Clemons is within walking distance of the marina around the bend. I ask, too, if they would recommend the restaurant they are going into.

"Oh, you can't go in there! That's a private club."

"We brought jackets and ties."

"Sorry. I suggest you guys go over to Bubba's. It's located just past the marina."

"We can take a hint. We're from Minnesota for crying out loud – we're not stupid."

"Half of the harm that is done in this world is due to people who want to feel important. They don't mean to do harm but the harm does not interest them." -T.S. Eliot, poet (1888–1965)

Continuing two hundred yards downstream, we find the marina pre-season empty. There is no one in sight except for a police car entering the adjacent parking lot. As we begin to make ourselves at home, I figure it would be better to get permission in this case rather than have to apologize later. I flag the policeman over to where we are getting out on the docks. The policeman is more than helpful. He contacts the marina owner and assures the person on the other end of the phone that the kayakers will not make a mess and will be gone first thing in the morning. He also says that he will let the next shift know they should give extra attention to the boats tonight. Before leaving though, he requests my full name, home address, phone number, and birth date. Luke tells Andy, "Evidently Jim's reputation precedes him."

"Ka-Ka-Ska-Ska"

"The worst of me is known, and I can say that I am better than the reputation I bear." -Johann Christoph Friedrich von Schiller, poet, dramatist and philosopher (1759–1805)

At the Hotel Clemons, we are greeted by Rude Girl, who couldn't care less if we stay here or not, so we leave and locate a smaller hotel eight blocks away. Tony went out ahead on a re-con and reports back that the clerk seems to be much friendlier. The place isn't as nice, however, and the rate is the same. We return to Rude Girl and interrupt the feud she is currently engaged in with her Aunt Merla who is sitting in an office thirty feet away from the front desk.

Hot showers are the first thing on the agenda. Then it is off to Bubba's where for a small up-charge everything on the menu can be "Bubba Sized." Bubba sizing is a good way to end a not-so-good day.

Over dinner, maps are studied and we learn that the river runs to the southeast from Hannibal for more than eighty miles. Then it runs to the northeast for only eight miles or so before going southeast again for another twenty-plus miles. The forecast is for the same ruthless 15–25 mph wind with gusts in excess of 30 mph, except tomorrow the wind is shifting and will go in the same direction as the flow of the river. It will be the first day of this outing without the persistent headwind. Everyone agrees on getting a record early start in the morning.

Thursday, April 12, 2007

It is a record – up at 6:00, breakfast, and on the water at 7:40. One hour later, we're seven miles downstream and going straight through Lock & Dam No. 22 without delay. The lock crew tells us that we are either extremely tough or extremely crazy. We confess that it has been the consensus of those encountered along the way that we are the latter.

"What sane person could live in this world and not be crazy?" -Ursula K. Le Guin, author (1929–)

Lock & Dam No. 23 has been decommissioned (a pleasant surprise) and Lock & Dam No. 24 is another straight shot through with no waiting. The afternoon tailwinds coupled with strong currents prove to be quite advantageous. Andy has his sail up and is able to tow Tony up to a speed of 10.1 mph.

A few miles upstream from Lock & Dam No. 25, Tony and I witness a mind-blowing incident. One of the green navigational buoys yields to the muscle of the river current and disappears below the surface for several minutes, then pops up again without warning. The process repeats two more times before we pass it. It's a scary thought, but "What would happen if we were paddling after dark and were on top of that thing when it popped back up?"

There is a brief holdup before entering Lock & Dam No. 25, providing a short rest and time to study the map. This appears to be the best option for a take-out today and a great place for Mark Scotch to join the troop. The secure recreation area next to the dam will be a safe place to park Luke's truck and trailer until Saturday when my nephews drive up from St. Louis to deliver it to the take-out.

We lock through and paddle around the far corner of the lock's retaining wall to a shallow backwater with an easy access to the road and parking area. Once on land, Mark is called. He's en route and says he will be here in an hour.

We've gone sixty-six miles in the past ten hours without getting out of the boats or taking time to eat much of anything except for a quick snack. The picnic area is flooded with about two feet of water, and the harsh northwest wind is whipping against our wet clothing. We take shelter in the entrance of the women's bathroom where I boil water for Ramen Soup.

"It is not the strongest of the species that survive, nor the most intelligent, but the one most responsive to change."
-Charles Darwin, naturalist and author (1809–1882)

Jason, the nightshift lock attendant, spots us as he is reporting for work. Instead of entering the security gate two hundred feet away, he swings around and drives over to the bathroom to introduce himself. Jason, not yet the age of thirty, is a diver for the Army Corps of Engineers and has served two tours in Iraq. He tells us that if we have time after dining, to come over to the gate and he'll give us a personal tour.

The tour includes an overview of the procedures and practices of the control room, all the mechanical workings of the operation, and a trip up on top of the deck above the dam gates. In parting, Jason tells us not to worry about the boats and gear for the night because he will make sure the main gate is secure.

It is around 7:00 when Mark arrives. Meanwhile, we find out that Troy, IL, the nearest town with any restaurants or hotels is fifteen miles west. Having the truck available tonight is a real benefit. We check into the Super 8 in Troy and order pizza.

Friday, April 13, 2007

The paddle begins at 9:50 this morning. The wind is neither benefit nor detriment and the scenery for the next fifty miles to Granite City, IL is virtually non-descript – more undeveloped floodplain.

We reach the confluence of the Missouri River and the mighty Mississippi late in the afternoon, the half-way point between the Headwaters and The Gulf. This particular spot along our route has been the topic of countless conversations since beginning the adventure at Lake Itasca. According to an article Vicki Bennington posted in the Illinois Business Journal on February 16, 2004, "At its confluence, the Missouri nearly doubles the volume of the Mississippi accounting for forty-five percent of the flow at St. Louis in normal times and as much as seventy percent of the flow during some droughts." From other stories read we know the waves at the confluence of these two great rivers can reach several feet high and create perilous eddies. As we approach with uneasiness, it becomes very obvious that this is going to be a major nonevent! Andy and I both check our GPS units to verify we are truly at the confluence. There is no question, we are here and there is absolutely nothing worth noting from where we sit, no mammoth waves, no unimaginable turbulence, and no colossal back-currents sucking us upstream to Wisconsin.

"A thing long expected takes the form of the unexpected when at last it comes." -Mark Twain, author and humorist (1835–1910)

This isn't the first time we've been duped by outrageous myths of the Mississippi. We have heard and read stories of violent whirlpools, measuring twelve to fifteen feet in diameter and as much as six feet deep, making even the most wild theme park ride seem like a merry-go-round in comparison. Then there are those paddlers who tell tales of menacing barge traffic barreling up and down river, creating vast rogue waves capable of swamping the Queen Mary II.

"Ka-Ka-Ska-Ska"

Well, either this exploration has traveled in some sort of fourth dimension known only in the Twilight Zone, or there's been a teeny-weeny bit of exaggeration on behalf of those who have traveled the river before us. We have, however, only by the Grace of God, narrowly survived countless attacks from gigantic and merciless pelicans flying in flocks numbering in the thousands. The only thing that drives these extraordinarily unnatural and brutally sadistic oversize birds of prey into a hateful frenzy more than the mere presence of a kayak is the sight of someone paddling a kayak. These lily-white feathered monsters swoop down out of nowhere on unsuspecting kayakers, pounding their ten-foot wings against the hulls of the small crafts, trying to capsize them so they can feed more easily on the defenseless paddler left adrift. It is believed that the peculiar and disgusting mustard-yellow knob resting on the beaks of these direct descendants of the pterodactyl is some sort of radar device used solely for the purpose of tracking their victims. Anyway... that's going to be the Itasca Kayakers' contribution to the book of Mississippi Legends and Myths.

"The difference between false memories and true ones is the same as for jewels: it is always the false ones that look the most real, the most brilliant." -Salvador Dali, painter (1904–1989)

It's a tough decision to leave the water at Granite City, IL. There are almost two hours of daylight remaining, but it is doubtful that there will be a convenient take-out downriver in close proximity to a motel. And being this close to St. Louis, there will definitely not be a place to camp. Besides, no one is looking forward to camping tonight considering the rain in the forecast.

One thought in the process is to leave the boats at Lock & Dam No. 27 four miles ahead and take a taxi from there to the nearest motel. I radio the lock crew and request a land-line telephone number in order to discuss the idea of leaving the boats under the watchful eye of the security cameras. The lock crew will have nothing to do with the additional responsibility. Within minutes, it begins to sprinkle, making the decision easier.

After dragging the boats up over the rocks onto the levee, we secure them with the cable lock beneath an overpass and walk the distance of a little over a mile to the Western Inn. Dinner is at a nearby place called "EAT HERE."

Saturday, April 14, 2007

The forecast was correct. The rain that began last night before dinner was finished is still coming down this morning. According to the man on the television, the rain will not stop until tomorrow. The weatherman also predicted it will be much cooler than the high of 40 F that was on yesterday's thermometer.

Breakfast is at the Waffle House next to the motel. There the GPS is scanned for a premium take-out that will end this week's trip. The take-out needs to be relatively easy to find both on land and water, as well as provide safe parking for the truck when the nephews drop it off. A school parking lot is selected near Cliff Park, located twenty-four paddle miles downriver.

While walking back to the boats, a sheriff's deputy stops long enough to inquire as to where we're going and what we're up to. Mark gives a quick explanation that tickles the deputy's funny bone. Standing there in pouring rain, again donned in life jackets and spray skirts with paddles hung over our shoulders, more than a half-mile from the river, we are beginning to understand what it is that people find so strange about the endeavor.

Everyone is soaked by the time we make it to the crest overlooking where the boats had been left. They're still here. "DANG!!!! We've gotta go ahead with this trip another day!"

"In some circumstances, the refusal to be defeated is a refusal to be educated." -Margaret Halsey, novelist (1910–1997)

At Lock & Dam No. 27, a green light is not seen on the approach, and the wind is blowing too hard on our back sides to take time to make a radio call. We are forced to turn about and take refuge behind a barge moored on the Illinois side of the river upstream two hundred yards. Sleet stings against our exposed skin as the determined wind gets in its last licks with a force that makes this the most difficult paddling yet over the past seven days.

In the shelter of the hull of the barge, I radio the lock and we wait. Fifteen minutes creep by before the green light comes on, giving us clearance to lock through. The lock is absolutely filthy with dead fish and floating debris everywhere. No one comes out for the usual small talk or to assist with our passage. When the horn sounds and the gates open, we are glad to have this one behind us for two reasons. The first reason is because it was so dirty and unfriendly. Secondly, this is the last lock on the river. The river is free flowing from here to the gulf, having dropped from 1,475 feet above sea level at Lake Itasca to the present elevation of 400 feet.

(St. Louis Arch)

Prior to the building of Locks and Dams on the Upper Mississippi, the river rapids north from this point prevented navigation for many large boats, making St. Louis a bustling boom town and inland port. By the 1830s, it was common to see more than one hundred fifty steamboats at the St. Louis levee at one time. By the 1850s, St. Louis had become the largest U. S. city west of Pittsburgh, and the second-largest port in the country, with a commercial tonnage exceeded only by New York. [9]

The next twenty miles is through the suburbs of St. Louis and downtown, past the world famous six hundred thirty foot tall Gateway Arch. The current is again strong, easily exceeding 6 mph. Good time is made as the rain lets up to what could be considered more of a drizzle or a heavy mist, depending on who is depicting the scene. Due to the strong current, the search for an opportunity to exit the river begins a half-mile before the waypoint marking where the truck is supposed to be parked.

There is a steep bank and according to the GPS, a road just beyond our line of sight. There is also a small creek coming in on the right that lures Tony and me from the main channel. It is passable around a few trees and through a culvert under the roadway above. Then the water becomes too shallow to paddle and we are forced to get out. We pull the boats through the remaining twenty yards of trickle and on up the grade, perhaps another hundred yards or so. Luke, Andy, and Mark found a different egress and negotiated the underbrush to the top of the hill. They arrive soon after Tony and me.

"What you do is of little significance; but it is very important that you do it." -Mohandas K. Gandhi (1869–1948)

The only car in the parking lot is backing up and going forward, backing up and going forward. Andy approaches the car and finds a young man who had recently acquired his driver's permit practicing basic maneuvers with his dad. Andy convinces the dad to give him a ride to the school parking lot, and is back fifteen minutes later.

After paddling 352.6 miles on this trip, it's time to make a trail for home, but first a stop at the arch for a tour and then dinner. We leave St. Louis behind at 6:00 with an 875 mile straight-through drive ahead of us.

Trip Report
- 1,172.1 miles completed (50.8% of total trip)
- 1,134.9 to New Orleans

[Leg 1]
St. Louis, MO to Wilson, AR; 367.2 River Miles

Friday, September 21, 2007

As usual, Andy, Luke, and I leave Grand Rapids on a Friday with departure time shortly after noon, stopping only for gas before picking up Tony in Moose Lake. All goes well until getting to the south side of Minneapolis. Luke is driving, keeping up with the 5:00 P.M. traffic when a motorcycle patrolman merges onto the freeway from the right. A few minutes later, Luke checks his rearview mirror, and the patrolman is behind with his flashing red lights on. Luke pulls over. No one has a clue what this could be about. A couple of possibilities are thrown out – maybe one of the boats is loose or on fire, or maybe the trailer lights aren't working.

The patrolman approaches the driver's side window.

"Do you know how fast you were going?"

Luke admits he has no idea. "I was just keeping up with the traffic."

"This is a 55 zone. I clocked you at 75 mph. Didn't you see me? You passed right by (whining voice). Then you kept on going (more than a whining voice). What does your driving record look like?"

"I think I had a ticket two years ago."

The patrolman leaves with Luke's license in hand.

Luke turns to the others in the truck, "How far back do you think his records will go? The last ticket I had was... maybe two years ago, but I had a real bad stretch right before that where I got three in one year."

Jim Lewis

The patrolman returns in a few minutes with Luke's award, "I gave you a break. I wrote it for 70 mph in a 55 zone. There is a telephone number on the back you can call to get more information regarding the amount of the fine."

"Thank you, officer."

Back into traffic again with yet another lesson learned… regardless how fast the traffic is going, do not pass a patrolman. One mile down the road, the speed limit increases to 75 mph. Andy calls the number on the back of the ticket. The fine is $137. Yep, we're off to an excellent start.

"Society prepares the crime; the criminal commits it."
-Henry Thomas Buckle, historian (1821–1862)

The twelve hour drive from Grand Rapids to St. Louis beginning eleven hours ago has stretched out beyond belief. After making more than a couple wrong turns navigating around Mason City, nearly running out of gas in a sea of corn fields in the dark somewhere in northern Iowa, wasting time to stop to eat at a bowling alley that advertised food on a large sign out front but inside the only thing found on the menu was popcorn, shopping at Wal-Mart, then dinner at a real restaurant – the foursome reluctantly gives in to exhaustion. We stop at a Comfort Inn on the outskirts of Cedar Rapids, IA with still three hundred miles to go!

I'm nominated to go in to negotiate an economical room rate and fail miserably. There is one room left at the cost of $99.00. The young lady behind the counter is not willing to lower the price, but I'm told there are more hotels a few blocks away that may be more in line with our budget. Before we get to the next hotel, Tony wakes up in the back seat and recalls he has a friend who lives here. He makes a quick phone call. Twenty minutes later and after a few more wrong turns, we are greeted by Tony's friend, Steve, who has plenty of room for us.

"Ka-Ka-Ska-Ska"

"Finish every day and be done with it. You have done what you could; some blunders and absurdities crept in; forget them as soon as you can. Tomorrow is a new day; you shall begin it serenely and with too high a spirit to be encumbered with your old nonsense." -Ralph Waldo Emerson, writer and philosopher (1803–1882)

Saturday, September 22, 2007

After getting on the road at 8:00 A.M., we make it to St. Louis in five hours in spite of more wrong turns. In St. Louis, we stop for my brother-in-law, Duffy. He will ride with us to the put-in, and then take the truck back to his house for the week. Next Saturday, Duffy will meet us at the take-out.

The temperature is in the mid 80s when we arrive at Cliff Park. The hill is no less of an incline than it was in April, however, the climb is longer due to the water level of the river being quite a bit lower – down as much as twenty feet. There is no easy trail to the river's edge. Several trips up and down the steep bank are required to haul the gear through thick foliage and underbrush. We get on the water at 3:00 P.M.

Two and a half hours later and sixteen miles down river, a runabout slows down beside us to get our story. Steve Singer, the boat's driver, extends an invite to stop for a break at the boat club in Crystal City around the next bend. This sounds like a good idea.

Getting out on the dock in the swift current is not the simplest of tasks, but it's accomplished without getting wet. Steve is there to meet us and offers a ride into town to get something for supper – another good idea.

After returning from the excursion into town, we visit with Steve until nearly sunset. Then we paddle another nineteen miles, making a total of thirty-five for the day. Camp is set up under a cloudless moonlit sky around 10:00 on a mysteriously flat sand-covered island. The boats are taken a good forty feet up from the water's edge, but the island is so flat, the boats are not much more than three inches above river. Farther from shore is not going to get them any higher. Hopefully, the water won't rise overnight or there will be more at jeopardy than just the boats.

Sunday, September 23, 2007

Before breaking camp, we do a little exploring. Luke estimates this island to be at least thirty acres. What a wonderful place to have camped and a great way to begin this trip!

(A new beginning)

"Ka-Ka-Ska-Ska"

Mid morning, we pass the confluence of the Kaskaskia River. I'm out front, and the first to see the huge brown sign with foot-high white lettering. Unfortunately, I can't seem to pronounce the name of the river correctly. I point it out to the others as "Ka-Ka-Ska-Ska." As a result, I become the butt of ridicule (again) and "Ka-Ka-Ska-Ska." becomes the universal catch phrase for almost everything...

"Ka-Ka-Ska-Ska." ("Look at the awesome sunrise/sunset.");
"Ka-Ka-Ska-Ska." ("A barge is coming!");
"Ka-Ka-Ska-Ska." ("Good coffee.")
"Ka-Ka-Ska-Ska." ("etc.").

"There is nothing more difficult to take in hand, more perilous to conduct, or more uncertain in its success, than to take the lead in the introduction of a new order to things."
-Niccolo Machiavelli (1469–1527)

We've been paddling against a 10–15 mph headwind since getting on the river this morning with the temperature rising to 91 F, according to the radio. It's noon and time for lunch as we arrive in Chester, IL, home of Popeye-the Sailorman, where a six foot, 900 lb. bronze statue stands in the *Elzie C. Segar Memorial Park* in honor of the cartoon character.

A fisherman near shore says there is a boat landing a few hundred feet down the river on the left and once on land, "… just follow the stair steps up the hill. It's an easy access to town."

The landing is simple to find and as the fellow said, there is a set of steps on the far side of the railroad tracks leading up the hillside. I count a total of 286. Tony and Luke both count 271. (I am getting so tired of being wrong all the time.) At the top of the hill, the first two eateries are closed because it is Sunday. Continuing the search for another six, maybe eight blocks farther, we come by a nursing home. There are two ladies sitting outside. Andy asks about a restaurant, or better yet, "Is your cafeteria still open?"

One of the ladies responds she's sorry, it has already closed and everything is cleaned and put away. The other woman mentions a place another half-mile away, and offers a ride. That sounds good, but when we get to her car, it is full of stuff and there is no room for any passengers. Not a problem, "We've walked this far, another ten minutes shouldn't be too bad." Amazingly, she is pretty accurate about the half-mile, and it's Marcello's Italian Café for lunch. The first thing ordered is a large pitcher of ice water, then a refill, followed by another. No one is too anxious about getting underway again. The lunch stop extends past two hours.

Whether it is because it's Sunday, or who knows what, the barge traffic is minimal today. We see only three moving upstream and none heading south. Ignoring the heat and the wind, paddling is done at a steady pace through the late afternoon and beyond sunset. Our stop for the night is on a sand beach below a private campground that overlooks the river from a small bluff. Prior to setting up, we hike up the hillside to the office. It closed an hour before.

On the way back down to the beach, we stop to talk with a couple, who are proud that they have had their camper set up at this same location for the past seven years. The lady tells us to go ahead and make ourselves at home on the beach. If anyone hassles you, "Tell 'em you're our nephews."

"Ka-Ka-Ska-Ska"

"Ka-Ka-Ska-Ska." ("It's good to have friends in high places".) The hot showers and campfire feel good after the fifty-one miles today.

"You have your brush, you have your colors, you paint paradise, then in you go." -Nikos Kazantzakis, poet and novelist (1883–1957)

Monday, September 24, 2007

We rise with the sun at 6:30 A.M. The beach looked so good last night, but trying to get ready for the day is another story. The soft fine sand brings its own set of problems. Andy asks, "Does anyone else feel like they have sand in their everywhere?" Seconds later, he drops his toothbrush and now claims he really does have sand in his everywhere.

"Sand...in your ears, your eyes, your bed, your food, your pipe, your shoes...You adjust to the fact of it, and move your feet slowly while cooking." -John Graves, author (1920–)

Ten miles or so downstream, we begin to paddle through the Trail of Tears State Park near Jackson, MO. The 3,415-acre park is a memorial to the Cherokee Indians, who lost their lives in a forced relocation during harsh winter conditions in 1838–39. The park is located on the site where nine of the thirteen groups of Indians crossed the Mississippi River. Thousands lost their lives on the trail, including dozens on or near the park's grounds.

While we are paddling along the face of a two hundred foot rock wall, a large tree at the base of the wall crashes to the ground. The echo off the wall above resonates like a dynamite explosion. Luke assures the others, "I am quite confident the same effect would have occurred in our absence."

Jim Lewis

"When the oak is felled the whole forest echoes with its fall, but a hundred acorns are sown in silence by an unnoticed breeze." -Thomas Carlyle, historian and essayist (1795–1881)

This is our third day on the river and the number of monarch butterflies is incredible – literally hundreds of them. It turns out that the section of river south of St. Louis to almost Memphis is a flyway for the butterflies' fall migration. The monarch is the only butterfly known to make a two-way migration the same as birds do. Unlike other butterflies that can survive overwinter as larvae, pupae, or even as adults in some species, monarchs cannot survive the cold winters of northern climates. Triggered by environmental cues, the monarchs know when it is time to travel south for the winter. Using a combination of air currents and thermals, the butterflies can cover long distances. Some fly as far as three thousand miles to reach their winter home in Mexico. Traveling between fifty and one hundred miles a day, it can take up to two months to complete their journey. The farthest ranging monarch butterfly recorded traveled two hundred sixty-five miles in one day. [9]

"Everyone is like a butterfly; they start out ugly and awkward and then morph into beautiful graceful butterflies that everyone loves." -Drew Barrymore, actress and film producer (1975–)

The temperature is close to what it was yesterday, if not a few degrees warmer. The wind is not a factor at all. Barge traffic has increased somewhat, though, providing more thrills than challenges. We find ourselves riding on four foot swells as eight to ten foot waves are churned up directly behind some of the barges. The largest barge seen is six containers wide and six deep. Our other excitement comes with the 'boils' and whirlpools. Boils occur when there is a sudden change in the river depth, usually caused by excessive erosion along the bottom. The result is the surface water begins to boil likened to the turbulence of a Class I or II rapids. Whirlpools, on the other hand, show up here and there for no apparent reason that we're aware of. They vary in size between ten and twenty feet in diameter. The kayaks track well through the whirlpools, sometimes dropping a few inches as we paddle over the center of the vortex. Neither the boils nor the whirlpools present the danger described by other paddlers. Some of the locals have told us that they will often take their small power boats out and intentionally stop in a whirlpool just to drift around in a circle for a while.

Today's lunch stop is in Cape Gerardeau, MO. The landing takes place on a muddy shoreline next to a construction site with a real crappy climb up a hill through grossly thick vegetation that appears to be ideal habitat for snakes and/or other creepy crawly undesirables. Luck is with us and there are no close encounters of any kind. Exiting the snarl of brush and thorns at the top of the incline, we find ourselves in the backyard of a hospital complex. There we walk around the compound of buildings and across the well-kept grounds. Then within two blocks, the landscape transforms to a myriad of dilapidated storefronts. Here skeptical eyes from shaded doorways give long and apprehensive stares at the oddly dressed foreigners in their midst who, by the way, are not wearing life jackets and spray skirts.

Jim Lewis

The friendly clerk at the gas station suggests lunch at an independent fast food drive-up three blocks away. After burgers and fries while sitting on a retaining wall, it's a stop at the local grocery store for supplies. Checking out, I'm given a choice of plastic bags: either the three cent bags or the slightly larger bags at a cost of six cents. I lean toward being frugal, and within five minutes of leaving the store, one of the bags breaks open. Of course I take slack for not springing for the more expensive bag.

"Thank everyone who calls out your faults, your anger, your impatience, your egotism; do this consciously, voluntarily."
- Jean Toomer, poet and novelist (1894–1967)

During the walk through the hospital parking lot on our return trip, a security cop follows us in his car for several minutes, staying at least two car lengths behind. At the end of the lot, we begin to cross the lawn. The Pinkerton turns and heads back the other way. It looks like he is going around the far side to cut us off. We arrive at the lower lot ahead of him and sit down on the curb to wait for his arrival. The expectation is that he will engage us in conversation. If things go in the right direction, we'll ask if it's possible to get some photos of a shirtless me, going spread-eagle over the hood of his squad car. This is something we regret not doing during the previous run-ins with Johnny Law.

It's not going to happen. The security cop shows up, sees us sitting there, quickly turns around and leaves without even making eye contact. Not to fret though. With this bunch, there will probably be more opportunities.

Instead of risking the hillside back to the boats, we take a longer route through the construction site.

"Ka-Ka-Ska-Ska"

About a mile out of Cape Gerardeau, we see a barge coming from behind. Andy is paddling on the very edge of the navigational channel, and is quite a ways out in front of the barge when the captain sounds the horn once. Then a few moments later, he follows with five short blasts. This is the signal for, "Something really bad is definitely going to happen. Get out of the way NOW!" Andy holds his own. The channel is definitely wide enough. There is no need to move. A couple minutes pass and the horn sounds another series of five short blasts. Andy, being a sailor, explains that using the horn is much more effective than trying to fling a black cat across your bow. Nevertheless, this horn honking business doesn't do anything but annoy Andy, who quickly makes his own opinion known. His outburst has no visible impact on the barge whatsoever. It keeps coming, and passes by at an extremely safe distance.

We drop in behind the barge and follow it the next five miles. Then going into a sharp right-hand bend, the barge doesn't even attempt the turn. It heads straight towards the shore. Luckily, it stops short of going aground, but now has to go in reverse and jockey back and forth to swing the thing around the corner. "Ka-Ka-Ska-Ska." ("Nice driving, Sport.")

"Life is an adventure in forgiveness." -Norman Cousins, author and editor (1915–1990)

An hour passes and the same barge is again coming up fast. This time, we all give him plenty of room to avoid another horn incident. Almost immediately after it passes, it slows to match our speed. Nearing dusk, the running lights are as welcome as is his draft. We stay with him until 8:30, and then find a nice place to camp on a long sand island, after logging in an excellent fifty-two miles. No hot showers tonight, but there is another fine campfire.

Tuesday, September 25, 2007

Having a full moon usually means a high pressure system and clear skies, however, the forecast calls for rain and a strong storm front moving slowly through the area today and tomorrow. We get up early and pack quickly to keep things dry as long as possible. A light rain begins to fall soon after our start down the river.

The weather continues to be monitored on the marine radio. Over the next three hours, the light rain ramps to intermittent but heavy downpours. Then the lightning begins. First, the strikes are visible only on the distant horizon. The accompanying thunder that trails by several seconds prompts a move closer to shore, just in case an exit is required. This proves to be a smart maneuver. A lightning strike hits within a hundred yards or so on river-left. This time, there is no lapse of time between the flash and the thunder. Tony, Luke, and Andy run their boats up on the soft sand and dash for cover. As if having practiced the maneuver many times, Tony jumps out of his boat as soon as it hits land, drags it a few yards, flips it over on the beach, and somehow manages to snake his way up inside. Luke and Andy duck into some underbrush away from any large trees. I, on the other hand, choose to stay put on the water and hunker down as low as I can in the cockpit. My assumption is that the lightning will find somewhere else to touch the earth.

"Patience is also a form of action." -Auguste Rodin, sculptor (1840–1917)

"Ka-Ka-Ska-Ska"

Ten minutes pass and the rain continues to fall in buckets, but there is no more thunder – at least not until Tony sticks his head out from his plastic cocoon, then CRACK!!! And it's back inside for another ten minutes. By now, the rain has subsided, and all three on shore emerge from their refuge. The beach, slick with mud, makes a dandy place to run and slide. Luke and Tony do not let the opportunity pass.

(Slip-slidin')

Afterward, when talking about how none of us had ever seen it rain so hard for so long. Tony says, "Had we been in a survival situation, it would have been a great chance to have been able to collect water."

Andy's response, "I think I did collect some... in my underpants."

In spite of an early start today, only thirty-three miles have been paddled by 1:30 when we arrive at Wickliffe, KY. No excuses, it's just the way it is. The plan is to find a place for lunch, monitor the weather, and determine if it's best to continue on or stop for the day.

Like so many of the river towns, Wickliffe is all but gone. The only restaurant we find is a gas station that has a deli area and a couple of booths.

Two hours pass since our arrival. Most of this time has been spent overlooking the river from the protection of a pavilion near the landing even though the welcome sign above the entrance states, "NO LOITERING." Incidentally, the sign is garnished with no fewer than eleven bullet holes.

The in-between-storms sky hangs heavy with grey clouds, producing a downright gloomy and depressing panorama. Light under the roof of the small pavilion is minimal. All sitting at one of the two tables, my three companions are deep in conversation on their cell phones. All have their backs toward me. I am seated more behind than off to the side, at the other table. It looks like one of those photos you see in Life magazine where the subjects are lost in a world without color. I take out my camera, compose an award winning shot, and snap. Thinking the flash from the camera is a lightning strike, they all jump like little school girls. "Ka-Ka-Ska-Ska." ("Woops. Sorry, I didn't really mean for that to happen." :-)

"Happiness lies in the joy of achievement and the thrill of creative effort." -Franklin D. Roosevelt, 30th President of the U.S.

"Ka-Ka-Ska-Ska"

Tony contacts his brother back home to have him check things out on the computer. The report comes back that the storm is not going to get any better. According to Google Earth, the next chance for sleeping under a roof is about twenty-five miles downstream where it looks like there's a barn near the river. The decision does not come easily but it's four to zero in favor of safety and comfort. The Wickliffe Inn is close to a mile away, about a block beyond the gas station where we ate earlier. We secure the boats, take whatever is necessary, and go for another hike.

Upon arrival to check in, we are told, "There is no room in the Inn." I plead with the lady-owner-operator of this twenty unit motel, but she insists that every room is taken due to a large construction project going on at the local paper mill. After fifteen minutes of me telling the poor lady about the lack of campsites in the immediate area, no other towns nearby, no options at all for lodging, the pending storm, the possible perils connected with camping in the wind, rain, and lightning, and suggesting that she may even consider letting us sleep in her lobby or in the laundry room, she finally caves and confesses. There is actually one room available. "I've been working hard all day and I'm just too tired to clean it."

"Give me the cleaning materials and the fresh linens, and I'll take care of it myself." She agrees and gives up the room for $40.00. "Ka-Ka-Ska-Ska.." ("Praise God for Dale Carnegie.")

After we've settled in, neighbors Joe and Steve, who are millwrights working on the construction project, drop in for a visit. Neither Joe nor Steve possesses a valid driver's license as a result of recent DUI's. That doesn't stop them from jumping in their pickup truck with an open beer to give Andy a ride to the store for supplies. Later, Steve provides another ride to the grocery store so we can buy steaks to be cooked on their grill.

While grilling, another of the neighbors stops over, "Just call me 'Biggun' – everybody does." Biggun is a welder with the railroad and proud of his 325 lbs, after having been on carrot & celery diet for the past few weeks. He brought with him a large of bottle of whiskey, "You boys are going to have a drink with me."

"Never refuse to do a kindness unless the act would work great injury to yourself, and never refuse to take a drink... under any circumstances." -Mark Twain, author and humorist (1835–1910)

Biggun apologizes for it being a cheap brand. He says that whenever people ask him why he doesn't spend a little more to get the quality blend, he tells them, "When you drink two and a half gallons a week, a feller just can't afford the expensive stuff."

I offer Biggun one of the steaks, but he declines, "I can't eat on an empty stomach."

Wednesday, September 26, 2007

We are on river at 9:00, facing a 15–20 mph headwind. We're bounced around pretty good for the next six hours and thirty-two miles before arriving at Hickman, KY. Along the way, we encounter a two mile stretch of barges moored on river's edge and do our best to carry on bits of conversation with the work crews as we pass.

Hickman is a mile upstream on a small river with virtually no current to speak of, making the side trip relatively easy. The landing is close to being knee-deep mud, but it's better than getting out on rocks and fast water any day. An old man with a canoe has a tent set up on shore. He's making his way downriver for the winter, taking his time, camping and staying with friends whenever possible.

Lunch is at the Mengo Mart, another gas station restaurant. Everyone orders the half-pound Redneck Burger with fries which turns out to be a mighty fine meal. Back at the landing, there are two guys sitting in a flat bottom boat waiting for a friend who is coming to give them a lift. I ask if they had been out fishing.

"No, we were working on the river helping with the dredging."

The pair in the flat bottom goes on to tell the story of having their boat flip over while being towed by one of the Coast Guard tenders. In the process, they lose the shroud from their motor. Not a good day for them, but it is good for us to have them here at this time. They are willing to help stabilize each of the kayaks as we push off. One of the guys asks, "You ever hunt for your own food and cook it on an open fire?"

"No, although we have talked about it."

"That's what I like to do – kill things and cook them over the fire. I really like to do it to squirrels and deer. You ever run into water moccasin or cotton mouths?"

"No, although we have talked about it. Ah...Thanks for help. Hope you have a better day tomorrow." (We're not much for conversation at this time.)

Later in the afternoon, we startle eleven wild turkeys feeding along the river causing them to scurry off into the woods. "Now, there's something that might taste good cooked over an open fire."

Around the next bend, is a flock of pelicans, perhaps a hundred or more. "Probably wouldn't be good cooked in any way."

"Hunting is not a sport. In a sport, both sides should know they're in the game." - Paul Rodriguez, stand up comic (1955–)

Between the earlier headwind and the less than anticipated river current, our fun-meter is once again pegged. We settle for forty-five miles instead of the fifty-plus that we had hoped to do. We're off the river, setting up camp on a mile-long sandbar at 7:00 during the dwindling remains of today's sunshine. One more factor in the decision to exit early tonight is the news of another storm front coming in.

Coyotes watching from the shadows on the far side of the sandbar begin to chant as we make ourselves at home. It could be the coyotes are saying these strangers are welcome, but I doubt it.

Rain drops begin falling while we pitch our tents. It's not enough to stop us from going ahead with a good size campfire, thanks to the abundant supply of dry driftwood. The fire is stoked one more time before bidding each other goodnight at 9:00. The storm hits without compassion at midnight, letting loose with a deluge of rain and heavy winds. It continues throughout the rest of the night. Then, as quickly as it started, it stops as morning breaks with a brilliant sunrise. The stormy night made for poor sleeping conditions, especially for Tony whose tent collapsed around him under the force of the winds.

"Sunshine is delicious, rain is refreshing, wind braces us up, snow is exhilarating. There is really no such thing as bad weather, only different kinds of good weather." -John Ruskin, author, art critic, and social reformer (1819–1900)

"Ka-Ka-Ska-Ska"

Thursday, September 27, 2007

The morning events seem to be almost choreographed. The rain stops, the sun rises, each of us exit our tents at the same time, and though there's minimal conversation as things are packed, everyone suits up and simultaneously settles down in the cockpits. When we are no more than ten yards from shore, the coyotes start harmonizing once more. Their world is back to the way it was before the paddlers interrupted the serenity.

"What sets a canoeing [kayaking] expedition apart is that it purifies you more rapidly and inescapably than any other travel. Travel a thousand miles by train and you are a brute; pedal five hundred on a bicycle and you remain basically a bourgeois; paddle a hundred in a canoe {kayak} and you are already a child of nature." -Pierre Elliott Trudeau, politician, writer, constitutional lawyer, prime minister of Canada (1919--000).

The river is flowing faster today. It is at least 4.5 mph, and to help matters, we get into the draft of two barges running downriver. We remain there for the next ten miles.

We're in New Madrid at noon after twenty-two miles. The city's boat ramp is too steep to use, so we drag up in the mud next to it. Andy asks two fishermen, who are loading their boat onto a trailer, if there is a restaurant nearby. They recommend The Grill, located downtown a mile away, and offer a ride in the back of their pickup. We are appreciative of the lift and the recommendation. Once again, the food is great.

After lunch, there's some shopping to do. First, at the convenience store for supplies, then Andy makes a stop at an

-antique store. He knows he would be sleeping better if he had a decent pillow so he's going to see if they will sell him one. The antique store lady listens to his story and says she can't sell him what he wants. She is willing to give him one along with a pillow case. "Ka-Ka-Ska-Ska." ("Life is good!")

Luke also makes a quick stop at the local museum to check out their bathroom. When he joins us again, he says it was worth the $2.00 admission – into the museum, not the bathroom. He learned stuff too – in the museum, not the bathroom. The museum curator told him everything he wanted to know about the earthquakes, which the city is known for.

On December 16, 1811, the four hundred residents of New Madrid were jolted out of their beds at two in the morning by a violent earthquake. Massive cracks split the ground, and as the tumult continued, waters of the Mississippi rose and fell like a tide. Huge waves swept north, giving the impression that the river was actually flowing backwards. Boats were engulfed, capsized, and many of their crews drowned. The earthquake on December 16 was the first in a series of four. The second shock took place only hours after the first. A third quake shook the area on January 23, and a fourth, the biggest of all, occurred on February 7. The last one hit an astounding 8.0 on the Richter scale. Between the major quakes, there were thousands of aftershocks. The fault is believed to generate a slip every 250 to 400 years. "Ka-Ka-Ska-Ska." ("That's scary stuff!")

"There are two big forces at work, external and internal. We have very little control over external forces such as tornadoes, earthquakes, floods, disasters, illness and pain. What really matters is the internal force. How do I respond to those disasters?" -Leo Buscualia, author, motivational speaker, and professor (1924–1998)

The visit to New Madrid lasts two hours. The break from the heat is energizing. We don't stop until we hit sixty miles for the day. Camp is set up under a dramatic full moon that illuminates the vast hard sand beach throughout the entire night.

Friday, September 28, 2007

Caruthersville, MO is only a few miles away and the selected target for breakfast. As we near the edge of town, a fellow working on a moored barge says there is a good landing on the other side of the casino, a half-mile downriver. Either we misunderstood or he was mistaken. Regardless, the landing isn't there. We end up paddling back upstream to search for something suitable. Again, we disembark on a miserably steep hill and climb through and over thick undergrowth that hides what no one wants to see.

The security person at the casino tells us that the restaurant on board doesn't open until 11:00. Not wanting to wait two hours to eat, we ask for other options. She says there is place about four or five blocks down the road called The Roundhouse Café. It turns out to be closer to fourteen or fifteen blocks but we make it – once more, certain that lesser men would not have survived nor would we survive very long if we were to eat this way everyday. The 'Hungry Man Special' includes three eggs, three strips of bacon, three sausages plus a side of biscuits and gravy. Waddling out of the Roundhouse, we cross the street to a convenience store for more supplies and then back to the river.

The rest of the afternoon goes by without much of anything happening. It's easy going as a respectable tailwind fills the sails carrying the kayaks along at 5–5.5 mph for a few miles anyway. At one point, the river is nearly one and three-quarters miles wide without any dams. Considerably different from the Headwaters where either shore line was often times within reach of a paddle.

After fifty-four miles logged, we stop for the night a few minutes before sunset on another driftwood-littered sand bar. There is no question that the fire tonight would be the envy of any Texas A&M fraternity.

"Driftwood marks the shore; the alphabet of ancients writing a last word." -Daniel Smythe, poet (1908–1981)

(Time to call it a day)

Saturday, September 29, 2007

The plan for the day is to go another twenty-four miles and call it a trip. I've identified a landing on the GPS that should be an easy access for the kayaks, as well as Duffy when he arrives with Luke's truck. I make a phone call giving him driving directions and set the rendezvous for noon.

Arriving at the proposed take-out thirty minutes ahead of schedule, everything looks good from the river. Once on land, we discover that in all likelihood, the last one to drive down the access road was someone taking their brand new 1954 Buick out for spin. "Ka-Ka-Ska-Ska." ("#@!*&%$#@!").

The kayaks are launched again and a new strategy is developed while we make a few more miles. According to the GPS, the next boat landing is located near Cash Road, south of Wilson, AR thirteen miles downriver. That's the first problem. The second problem is that cell signal has been lost. Duffy is still heading for the first landing. Fortunately, two guys in a small power boat are interested enough in what we are doing to stop and visit. The guys in the boat have real maps and are willing to go out ahead in search of other possible options. They disappear. The boaters return later with news that the only landing with a decent road access on the Arkansas side is the same one indicated on the GPS. Getting out on the Tennessee side of the river is out of the question. That would add several additional hours of driving to make the crossover.

I keep checking for a cell signal, and after a while, I am able to get through to leave a voice mail with rather sketchy instructions on the change of plans. Hopefully, Duffy will pick up the message before attempting the first meeting point. More than three hours have gone by since the first shot at getting off the river. We have yet to make actual contact with him.

From the river, the boat landing at Cash Road doesn't look any better than our first choice but we're willing to give it a try.

The guys in the power boat wish us well and before leaving, ask, "Have any of you been to Arkansas before?"

"No."

"Have y'all got a gun?"

"No."

"Good luck."

"Ka-Ka-Ska-Ska." ("What in the Sam Hill is that supposed to mean?")

Similar to other boat landings along the river, it is situated at the bottom of a steep hill, making it nearly impossible to carry the loaded boats to the top. It looks as if this landing has not been used in years either. We find it worth the time to clear away some of the rocks and dead wood to make a trail. It's better than having to step over the debris with each trip up and down. Andy volunteers to go in of search for the main road and hopefully a better cell signal while the other two and I cart the gear the hundred yards up the forty-five degree incline to the summit. It's exhausting work as each of us make at least five trips in the 90+F heat.

Another problem rears its ugly head. There is no more drinking water, PowerAde, or anything else to quench our thirst. Having made the assumption we would be off the river by noon, we failed to plan ahead for this fiasco. Tired and parched, we take refuge in the shade at the top of the hill, while waiting for word from Andy.

"Assumptions are the termites of relationships." -Henry Winkler, actor (1945–)

The perfect plan continues to unravel like a home-knit mitten caught on a barbed wire fence. The landing we have chosen appears to be on private property. There is an older structure that at one time must have been someone's house. Another fifty yards upriver is an additional building. From what can be seen without covert reconnaissance, it looks well maintained and inhabited. No one is about to go knocking on doors. Our faith rests in Andy trying to locate Duffy in a timely manner.

Zoom in on Duffy... After having picked up the message I left earlier, Duffy has been more or less driving blind. He's been heading south, staying close to the river. He stopped in Osceola to ask about boat landings, and was told the only landing that came to mind was on Island 35, a few miles downstream from where the kayakers are actually located. With no other information, that is where he headed. He encounters the same set of circumstances as the paddlers. It's all private land between the main highway and the river. Duffy spots a man coming out of one of the side roads and asks him if he had seen four kayakers come off the river.

"Nope. And if they did come off down hea, you better find 'em and get 'em outta hea befoe dawk or we'll eat 'em."

"Okay then. Thanks for your help."

Duffy decides to look elsewhere, seeing how he's not sure what to make of that conversation, or in other words, "Ka-Ka-Ska-Ska." ("What in the Sam Hill is that supposed to mean?") More miles down the road, he makes contact with another local. He poses the same question as before. The dialogue is different this time.

"Nope, ain't seen no kayakers. They probably got off the river up near Cash Road. There's an old boat landing there."

"All right, I'll try there. That's much better information than your neighbor gave me." Duffy shares the exchange he had with the first guy.

"Where was that?"

"Back that way about three miles."

"Oh yea. He probably meant it too."

Duffy has no response, but in all likelihood was thinking…
"Ka-Ka-Ska-Ska." ("Holy Crap!")

It's at this time that he gets a call from Andy.

From Andy's point of view… The good news is that he manages to talk with Duffy on the phone, and is able to provide some general directions toward our location. The bad news is that he has found this property fenced, gated, and surrounded by a deep ditch that during the rainy season would be considered a moat. There are not many options to getting the truck and trailer around the obstacles and closer to the river. Andy figures he is about a mile from where the rest of the gang is hiding out.

Shift back to the landing where Tony, Luke, and I are waiting… Over on the driveway fifty yards away two kids on four-wheelers come from the direction of the newer house. The one in the lead eyes the three kayakers and the pile of gear. He dynamites the brakes and skids to a halt. The kid trailing behind is gawking in the opposite direction and doesn't see that his pal has stopped until it's almost too late. It is a good thing the little guy has excellent reflexes. Somehow he manages to avoid a rear end collision that would not have turned out to be a pretty sight. The two kids point, talk between themselves, and move back toward the house. Minutes later a pickup truck emerges from behind the house – headed towards us.

"Oh, Oh."

Big guy gets out of truck. "How's it goin'?"

"Not so good…" (The story of our trip down river is told in the shortest form possible.)

Big guy spits, bites the inside of lip, and cautiously ponders what he has been told. Finally, after an extremely long uncomfortably awkward gap in time (just short of eternity), he extends his baseball-glove-size hand and says, "My name's Matt. Ya'll interested in a beer?"

"Yes Sir!" (In unison, like little kids responding to "Do you want ice cream?")

Matt has come prepared. In the back of his truck is a cooler the size of a beaver dam, filled with beer swimming in a pond of ice. There are few things better in this world than a new friend who brings beer on a hot day.

"Life consists in what a man is thinking of all day." -Ralph Waldo Emerson, writer and philosopher (1803–1882)

Matt says that he and his dad lease this land – 2,300 acres –for hunting and the only road into the place is gated and locked. This comes as a surprise; remember we three guys don't know anything about the gate business. Soon Matt is enlightened about Andy, Duffy, Luke's truck and the trailer. At first it is unclear if he is willing to unlock the gate or not, but as the conversation continues it becomes more obvious that he's feeling less threatened by our presence. After we have relieved the world of a spare twelve-pack between us, I turn the focus again on the subject of Andy, Duffy, Luke's truck and the trailer.

"Oh yeah… let me run down and get that gate open for them."

Ten more minutes pass and three pickups are coming back up the dirt road; one of them is the one we have been looking for, another is Matt's, and the third belongs to Matt's dad, Mike, who had come by about the same time Matt arrived at the gate. The time is now 5:00 and it looks like everything will work out just fine. More beer, more stories, more getting acquainted, and then it's time to load up and say, "Hope to see ya again."

Duffy has a question, "Luke, how many miles can you drive after the low fuel signal comes on?"

"It depends. Let me look." He checks the read-out on the dash. "My best guess is that we can make it about six, maybe eight more miles. How far is it to the nearest gas station?"

Matt, "Eleven miles."

Mike, "Have we got any gas here Matt?"

"Nope."

"Don't you boys worry. We'll take care ya. Follow me."

We thank Matt one more time for all he's done for us.

"We southern boys treat you Yankees pretty good, don't we?

"You sure do."

"Ya. We're always hopin' it'll rub off."

"We do, too."

Mike leads the way to his house in Wilson, a little over four miles away. There he produces a five-gallon gas can and pours it in. Keeping in form with the standard of hospitality he and Matt have already shown the Yankees, Mike refuses to take any money.

"Like cars in amusement parks, our direction is often determined through collisions." -Yahia Lababidi, writer (b. 1973)

"Ka–Ka–Ska–Ska"

At last we're on the way home with the only stop being to drop Duffy off at his house. We arrive in Grand Rapids at noon the next day.

Trip Report
   - 1,539.3 miles completed (66.7% of total trip)
   - 767.7 to The Gulf

[2008]

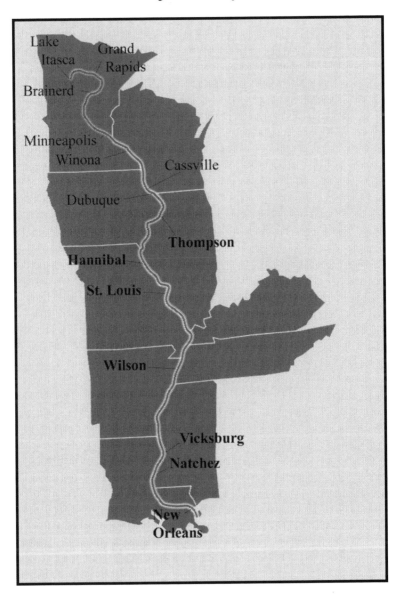

"Ka-Ka-Ska-Ska"

2008 Introduction

The Itasca Kayakers were together on the water sixty-nine times in 2007 logging in 6,314 miles as a group.

Personal updates:

- I continue to enjoy retirement.
- Luke has relocated to Duluth.
- Andy and Niccole are dating (see Minneapolis to Winona trip).
- Tony and Chandra have their wedding planned for August of this year.

Another exciting update. Beginning in December, 2007, work began to make the last leg of the adventure from the Headwaters to the Gulf a fund raiser for the American Cancer Society. It was Luke's idea and a great idea indeed. By the time of our scheduled departure in mid-April, we had raised over $9,000!

"Keep your eyes open, hold tight to your convictions, give it all you've got, be strong, courageous, and do everything in charity." -1Cor 16:13–14 (paraphrased)

Wilson, AR to Nowhere

Logistics for this excursion are a touch more complex than previous trips due to two key factors. First, I will be on vacation in Florida up to three days prior to the launch. Secondly, the other three (Luke, Andy and Tony) are planning to fly down to Memphis the evening before going on the water. This means the gear will have to be packed, delivered and staged ready-to-go in Memphis when everyone arrives. To complicate matters even more, Andy and Tony will be exiting the river at Vicksburg, MS instead of going all the way to the Gulf with Luke and me. Andy and Tony will finish at a later date. Oh, then there's the fact that we will start out in the middle of nowhere, so there will have to be a means to secure the vehicle.

Details of **THE PLAN**…

- March 30: Sharron and I leave Grand Rapids, MN arriving in Memphis, TN on Monday, March 31 where we will drop the trailer and all the paddling gear off at a storage facility (already reserved). We will continue on to Florida for two weeks, returning to Memphis on April 16.
- April 17: Sharron drives me to the put-in. The put-in is a boat landing on the Tennessee side of the river, a few miles west of Tipton, but directly across the river from Wilson, AR. I will paddle the thirty-something miles to Memphis.
- April 18: Sharron flies home to Hibbing, MN where she will connect with Luke. He will be getting on the same plane she is getting off. She will take Luke's truck for the next two weeks. Meanwhile, in Duluth Andy and Tony board a plane. The first connecting flight for Luke, Andy, and Tony is in Minneapolis, MN where all three will fly together to Memphis, arriving at 8:50 P.M.

- April 19: I drive the other three to the put-in so they can paddle to Memphis. I will meet them on the river in Memphis when they arrive at Mud Island Park, return the car and the trailer to storage, and take a taxi back to the river, at which time the four Huck Finn-wannabes will continue south.

- April 26: We arrive in Vicksburg. Tony has arranged for a friend of a friend to meet us at the casino on the river. This guy is not only willing to haul and store Andy's and Tony's boats and stuff, but will also drive them to the bus depot so they can get over to Jackson, MS to catch their flight home. Luke and I will continue on downstream.

- May 2: Sharron and Luke's wife, Traci, fly from Hibbing, MN to Memphis. They pick up the car and trailer from storage, then drive south on I-55 to meet Luke and me somewhere to be determined.

- May 3: Trailer-pulling Ladies hook up with Kayak-paddling Guys. Luke and I should be near Venice, LA. Venice, located about one hundred miles south of New Orleans, is the last road access on the river. Mile Marker Zero is eleven miles farther. We will coerce some unknown boat owner at the marina to accept a very small fee and give a ride to our ladies, and follow Luke and me to the Gulf. The key here is to have the same boater give us a ride back upstream to Venice.

- May 4: Sharron and I abandon Luke and Traci in New Orleans. They will spend a couple days kicking back before flying to Hibbing. Sharron and I will drive home, but on our way will stop at Vicksburg to retrieve the other boats and gear.

The above changes slightly one week prior to the launch date when I am able to make contact with Brian Smith of Memphis. Brian's mother-in-law, who lives in northern Minnesota, told me about Brian having recently purchased a kayak. I e-mailed Brian to see if he wanted to paddle with us. His response was that he wasn't sure he was up to a long trip. He also seemed quite concerned about the flooding in the area. When he read the part about me planning to do the stretch from the put-in to Memphis alone, he suggested that he drive us to the river on our schedule, and he would make sure the car and trailer were returned to storage. I gladly accept his offer. (In 1978, Brian and his friends paddled the entire Mississippi.)

"Ka-Ka-Ska-Ska"

For those who require a more visual approach to the detail of the logistics...

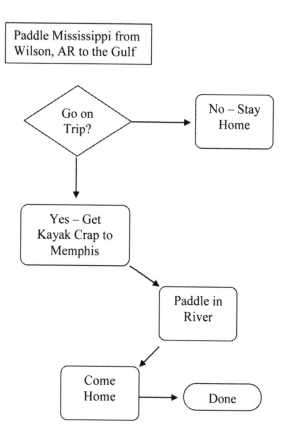

Brasington's Ninth Law: A carelessly planned project takes three times longer to complete than expected; a carefully planned one will take only twice as long.

Details of **REALITY**...

Sunday, March 30, 2008

All systems – Go. Sharron and I leave for Florida as planned, dropping the trailer at the storage facility in Memphis the following afternoon.

Saturday, April 5, 2008

In contrast to the eighty degree blue-sky Gulf Beach of Florida, a heavy snow begins to fall across Northern Minnesota, dropping a very wet twenty-four inches before Monday morning.

To the south, record one-hundred-year storms have plagued the United States south of the Mason Dixon Line through March and now into April. Flood levels of smaller rivers, such as the White River in Arkansas that flows into the Mississippi one hundred forty miles south of Memphis, are being featured daily on national news. Though water levels, floating debris, probable lack of comfortable camp sites, and the hazards presented while getting on and off the river are major concerns, Luke, Andy, Tony and I are still committed to beginning the trip in two weeks.

Friday, April 11, 2008

Another storm hits Grand Rapids, hurling down an additional ten to twelve inches of snow across the area. Winds in excess of 40 mph create snow drifts up to five feet causing the closing of area schools, colleges, shopping centers, medical clinics, and even sporting events. The forecast, is of course, for warming temperatures, assuring the white mass won't last long. It should melt within a few days. The run-off will join the waters of the already flooded Mississippi River Valley.

Monitoring the weather, we learn that Cape Girardeau, MO has received twenty-three inches of rain since March 1. It is close to twenty inches above year-to-date average. Mississippi dams from the Headwaters down to St. Louis are holding back as much river as they can.

Concern for the safety of the kayakers is mounting. Andy's mom and step-dad, who are vacationing in Arkansas, witness first-hand the swelling of the streams.

An excerpt from an e-mail Andy received today...

We're letting you know that the situation with the floods and overflowing rivers continues to be a serious problem down here. We received five or six inches of rain again a couple of nights ago and there is serious flooding going on along the White River near here. They keep talking on the TV about the levels being worse than back in 1982 when they had an all-time bad flooding situation. Also, they're talking about all of this water emptying into the Mississippi creating a dangerous situation. It's been raining a lot all along the areas in many states where it eventually ends up in the Mississippi.

So you guys should seriously check out the situation because according to the information we get down here, the Mississippi will become be a dangerous river with the excessive flowage.

Also, we went up to look at the White River yesterday and the river was loaded with piles of debris racing down the river. The current is unbelievably fast; huge trees, logs and junk going down the river. I can't describe how large these piles of stuff are. Also, there are campers, fifth-wheel campers, motor homes, vehicles, trucks, refrigerators, propane tanks, etc., going down the river. While we were looking at it yesterday, we saw a large fifth-wheel camper going down the river with only the air conditioner and top vents showing out of the water as it moved along. We saw it crash into the bridge and literally fly apart. There's probably so much more debris down in the water that we can't see.

It would be suicide to go down that river. I believe the worst is yet to come.

Hate to disappoint you, but you have to see it to believe what it's like. It's indescribable.

Love, Mom & Steve

After receiving the e-mail, Andy is able to contact Wayne Arguin, Chief of Prevention Dept. of the U.S. Coast Guard, stationed in Memphis. Wayne does not seem to be one who sensationalizes, but simply states the facts.

- The river is currently at thirty-seven feet and expected to rise another foot over the next ten days. The river at Natchez is over fifty feet at this time. Most Coast Guard personnel stationed in Memphis have not seen the river this high. Those who have seen these levels previously say that this time is much worse due to extended periods at low levels, allowing trees to grow on the banks. Now those trees are being "plucked" out and are rolling down the river.
- Two kayak/canoe races have been canceled along the river – one in Memphis and the other in Vicksburg.
- The river current is at 6–9 knots (7–10 mph) and causing navigational problems for barge towboats.

- Southbound barges are traveling 17 knots (nearly 20 mph) in some areas and under bridges to maintain control. Northbound barges are struggling to get 3 knots upstream.

- There are huge eddies near the banks with lots of churning water all the way across the river. Bridge areas are particularly dangerous, with exceptionally fast currents and large eddies on downstream side.

- The buoy recovery team commander called saying he was aborting recovery of buoys due to unsafe conditions.

- Earlier in the week, one of the USCG boats equipped with twin diesel engines was running at "three-quarter throttle" in order to maintain position while doing maintenance near a bridge.

- Emergency floodway "plugs" are being opened to relieve pressure towards New Orleans where the river is at sixteen and a half feet. Flood stage is seventeen feet.

Wayne tells Andy that he understands that the fast current alone isn't much of a concern, but the churning water, debris, eddies, lack of the USCG rescue launch site availability (the site is ten feet underwater) in addition to large storms and tornadoes do present a problem. He highly advises rescheduling this trip, "You can replace plane tickets."

Andy forwards the above information to the others saying, "This guy didn't seem like the doom and gloom soapbox show-boater with stories of 'giant eddies as big as your house' who made the trip down the Mississippi in 2007 and shared his journal on a blog site. Wayne comes across as being pretty rational and thought it would be a good trip at another time — not like the people who have said 'You're crazy.' or 'You guys sure are brave.'" Andy went on, "I'm not immediately saying we don't go but I need to pass this information on to you. I think we should discuss this."

Throughout the day, phone conversations volley between Andy, Luke, and Tony. They are not able to reach me until much later in the afternoon. Meanwhile, a "T" chart is being processed in everyone's mind weighing the pros and cons about going forward.

<u>Reasons for going forward include but are not limited to:</u>

1) Due to the fast current and not being able to exit along the way to camp each night, we could easily make the trip from Memphis to the Gulf in four, maybe five days at the most.

2) We could learn how to poop while in our boats, which in reality would probably be pretty easy — making it smell good would be the trick.

3) Even if we could find a place to camp, dry wood would be nonexistent, so we wouldn't have to waste time sitting around a campfire at night.

4) Going forward as planned could provide us with the opportunity of winding up on national news.

5) All the plans are in place. It would be a shame to have to go through getting the logistics ironed out for another trip.

6) We already have a lot of money invested in this trip. It would cost a few hundred dollars more to reschedule.

7) The temperature is ideal at this time of year. Later in the spring or summer, we may have to put up with seasonal heat.

8) Imagine all the good stuff we could find along the way – if only we had a place to stow it on board.

9) If the river is truly as bad as portrayed, we could encounter phenomenal perils that would win any "Phenomenal Perils Encountered Contest" hands down.

10) Paddling on water such as this would be a chance to prove to others that we truly are crazy.

<u>Reasons for not going on the trip at this time:</u>

1) None found.

Luke is finally able to reach me. We discuss the situation and agree to sleep on it before making the final decision.

"The whole problem with the world is that fools and fanatics are always so certain of themselves, and wiser people so full of doubts." -Bertrand Russell, philosopher, mathematician, author, Nobel laureate (1872–1970)

Saturday, April 12, 2008

Despite not being able to come up with one single reason for canceling the trip, it is decided to reschedule for another time – hopefully soon.

Monday, April 14, 2008

The Black River in Poplar Bluff, (SE) MO is breaking through levees. Temperatures across northern Minnesota are in upper sixties, making fast work of the snow.

Wednesday, April 16, 2008

Cassville, WI is mentioned on the morning news as a location where flooding has occurred. "There has been no forced evacuation at this time, but authorities are hoping people will get out before danger escalates."

While on the way through Memphis to recover the gear from storage, Sharron and I take a side trip to Mud Island Park on the Mississippi. This is a "don't miss" for anyone interested in the history of the lower Mississippi. While walking about the park, we are told of a large river cruise ship that came in earlier in the day. It had been traveling up from Louisiana for the past week, with three scheduled stops. Not one of the stops could be made due to the fact that there was no safe landing available where the ship could be moored. The ship was able to tuck in behind Mud Island to get the people off and onto buses to take them where they had to go.

My stomach creates eddies and turbulence of its own as I gaze at the river. The mighty Mississippi is as others have said – hard to describe, other than absolutely treacherous. There is no question that the right decision was to postpone the trip.

"Life is not measured by the number of breaths we take, but by the moments that take our breath away." -George Carlin, comedian (1937–2008)

Thursday, April 17, 2008

Sharron and I stop at the scheduled put-in just to see what it is like. The boat landing that we could see from the river last fall, with a parking lot all of forty feet above the water, is now level with the river. Only the very tops of the guard rail posts around the parking lot are visible.

Meanwhile, on the news it is reported that workers on an oil rig near Vicksburg, MS were given rides to work this morning on a power boat because of the flooding. In other news, the White River is expected to crest tomorrow.

Friday, April 18, 2008

Sharron makes it home as per the original schedule. (I do too, but low in spirit.)

Post script

Of all the folks we told about having to reschedule the trip, only one person calls the kayakers "chicken".

"You can safely assume that you've created God in your own image when it turns out that God hates all the same people you do." -Anne Lamott, writer (1954–)

[Leg 12]

Wilson, AR to The Gulf;
767.7 River Miles

Saturday, May 31, 2008

Having to reschedule the trip resulted in insurmountable logistical problems for Andy and Tony so, unfortunately they will not be on this trip. Luke and I will have to conquer the last leg of the river by ourselves. (Andy and Tony are planning to complete the trip in the fall.) Getting to and from is a little easier with only two paddlers, but having all four along would far outweigh any extra effort required in planning.

Sharron and I arrived in Memphis last Monday with the gear. Then we flew to Austin, TX to visit family for a few days. We returned yesterday and Sharron flew home this morning. Her return flight is scheduled for June 12, when she'll pick up the car and drive on down to the Gulf to meet Luke and me in Venice.

Luke was to fly into Memphis last night, but was delayed until this morning. To assure that he and I stay focused on the mission, Luke has a return flight from New Orleans on Sunday, June 15. About the only thing that has not changed too drastically from the original plan is the fact that Brian Smith is keeping the car at his house in Memphis after delivering us to the put-in.

Until this morning, Brian and I had never actually met or even talked on the phone. We have made all the arrangements via e-mail. Over the past month, Luke has been telling every-one, "Jim has a new best friend, Brian, who he met on the in-ternet." And then he is quick to follow up with, "The best part is that Brian still thinks Jim is a twelve year old girl."

After a few unexpected delays and a series of embarrassing wrong turns through a maze of narrow dirt roads, the kayaks are on the river at noon, heading towards the Gulf. The cur-rent is running strong though the volume of the river from Memphis on down to the Gulf is considerably less than what it was a month ago. It certainly appears to be much more navi-gable. According to the Coast Guard website, the river level at Memphis has dropped from thirty-eight feet to twenty-five feet, with the flow being reduced from 1300 kcfs (1000's cubic feet per second) to a flow of 800 kcfs. The change is typical of other locations downstream, except near Vicksburg and Nat-chez, where the river has settled in slightly below flood stage at forty-two feet and forty-eight feet respectively. The tempera-ture has gone in the opposite direction. Highs are predicted in the low to mid-nineties over the next ten days. Aside from the higher temperatures, another concern is whether we will have opportunity to replenish supplies. There are two sections of river below Memphis with one hundred fifty miles between bridges.

"Men build too many walls and not enough bridges."
-Isaac Newton, philosopher and mathematician (1642–1727)

(Put-in, north of Memphis)

Luke and I make excellent time (close to 7 mph), quickly closing the gap of the thirty-one river miles to Memphis. A mile upstream from Memphis, a call is made to Brian to give him a progress report. "That's good stuff. I'll be at Mud Island Park and give you a wave."

We pass by the park but are not sure if we can actually spot Brian on shore a quarter-mile away. There are a lot of people and the waving from the river is responded to by more than one person on land. We believe at least one of them has to be Brian.

A mile further, a police helicopter flies low overhead and the waving from us commences again. A minute later, a police boat approaches us from behind. The policeman standing on the bow is shouting, "Are you guys okay?"

"Yes."

"We got a report from someone in the park that you were waving and looked like you were in trouble."

"Nope. We have a friend who was standing on shore and we were waving to him."

It's not certain if the police are disappointed because there is no rescuing to be done or if they are skeptical of the truth. Either way they abruptly leave and do not even offer up a "Have a good trip."

"The greatest truths are the simplest: so likewise are the greatest men." -Augustus William Hare and Julius Charles Hare, Guesses at Truth, by Two Brothers, 1827

Soon after the police abort their mission, a small pleasure craft with a half-dozen youth aboard, approaches from outside the channel buoys on the right. Luke and I paddle over to visit. The teens are amused with the tale about the helicopter and the police boat. The conversation is cut short when we realize a barge, thought to have been parked near the bank on river-right, is swinging out. It's obvious that there is no thought or logic put into our decision of which way to turn. Both of us steer back across the channel in front of the oncoming barge, clueless as to how fast the current is taking us downriver or how fast the barge is closing in on us. Later, Luke told me that he was paddling for all he was worth when he looked up and realized he was so close to the front of the barge that he could not see the wheelhouse of the tow. Then he eyed me halfway between him and the barge. We make it, but I never want to be that close again! This is what bad dreams are made of.

"Reality is wrong. Dreams are for real." -Tupac Shakur, American rapper (1971–1996)

"Ka-Ka-Ska-Ska"

The lingering effects of last month's floodwaters are ever present: high water, strong current and plenty of floating debris. Over the next week Luke and I see everything from full length trees to smaller objects like a mounted automobile tire, a deflated basketball, tennis balls, Copenhagen tins, light bulbs, and dozens of empty soda bottles (green out-numbering other colors four to one). Believe it or not, the most frequent item seen is applicators for feminine products. And though there are many glass jars, only one has contents. It's a jar of olives – probably from a barge crew making "beertinis" after a long day's work. The most dangerous thing is a hypodermic needle floating near the surface, missing Luke's arm on a paddle-stroke by only three inches. Time and time again our paddles strike something under the surface, sometimes solid and other times more mushy than not.

"The river does not swell with clear water." -Italian proverb

We want to make as many miles as possible during the safer daylight hours, so there are no breaks taken throughout the afternoon other than an intermittent gulp of water. The exit from the river today is at 7:00, an hour before sunset, on a not-so-flat sand beach after forty-nine miles. "Ka-Ka-Ska-Ska." ("That's not bad for having such a late start this morning.")

[As final plans for this trip fell into place, Luke and I were concerned about being out of shape for any long distance paddling so we set out three weeks ago on a two day sixty-two mile trip

from Red Wing to Winona. It was the last section Luke needed to make up. Fellow club member Ed Murray joined us. We camped on Friday night and got out early the next morning. By noon, we encountered strong headwinds as we paddled from one end of Lake Pepin to the other. Before we reached the far end, it began to drizzle. We locked through Lock and Dam No. 4 in Alma, WI, not much before dark, as the rain continued. With twenty-two miles to go, it was either pull over and camp in the rain or push on to the end. We decided to finish the entire sixty-two miles and drive back home that night. The trip took sixteen hours and Luke and I didn't get out of our boats once. After that little outing, we knew we were ready for the last leg of the Mississippi and should be able to handle whatever comes up.}

Sunday, June 1, 2008

It's up at 5:00, oatmeal for breakfast, and on the water at 6:30. A whitetail deer is at the campsite to see us off, under blue skies and a temp of 70 F. Soon after getting on the water, I pass a fire extinguisher floating bottom side up on its way south. It is one of those shiny steel water air-charged extinguishers like I saw late yesterday. In all likelihood, it's one and the same.

Luke and I decide on a little different paddling strategy so as not to burn out. We will paddle hard for an hour and drift for ten minutes, repeating the routine throughout the day. It seemingly works well, and by 2:00, we have gone almost fifty-seven miles. Meanwhile, the skies have gone from blue to gray. Storm clouds are moving in from the southwest. There is no better time than now for lunch. The map indicates a boat landing up ahead on river-right, at the town of Helena, AR.

From the river, it looks like there's a park on the upstream side of the landing. Some folks are walking along a pathway. Two women see the kayaks and stroll out on the observation platform that stretches thirty feet out over the bank. Once they're within earshot, "Is there a place to eat within walking distance?"

"No."

"Is there a boat landing?"

"Yeah, but ya gotta go around, (Lady starts waving her arm in a repeated fashion showing the way)... like a circle."

Second lady, "Yeah. Go around, (replicating the same motion with her arm)...like a circle."

Luke and I have a good grasp on the idea and continue another hundred yards to a small stream that looks like it will lead to the boat landing. At the mouth of the stream are two fishermen in a flat bottom boat anchored up under the trees overhanging from shore. (All this is on river-right – the town of Helena, the park, the landing, and the fishermen with their backs to the shore and their lines stretched out toward the center of the main river channel.)

My theory is that you can never ask an important question too many times, especially if you have yet to get the answer you're looking for, "Is there a restaurant close by?"

"No, but we can give you a fish if you want something to eat."

"Ah..., thanks, but no thanks. We were hoping to get someone else to do the cooking today."

"Can't help ya there."

The landing is only a few minutes away. There is another guy pulling his boat out. The line of questioning begins again. (Hmm...doing the same thing, but expecting different results. What does that say about us?)

This guy at least puts some thought into our question, before he points to a building across the narrow waterway, "That was a restaurant. It's closed now. (pause...) There's another one on the other side of town, but that's about fifteen miles away."

A lady comes up from the landing and chimes in, "There's a casino across the river that serves food."

"Where?"

"Right over there."

Sure enough, [directly across the river] it's there alright —
with a great big red roof covering close to ten acres of one-
armed bandits, right in front of God, those two fishermen in
the boat, and everyone else!

"Ka-Ka-Ska-Ska." ("WHAT?!! There's a casino directly
across the river?!!")

We get back in the kayaks and cross over, a distance of a little
more than a half-mile. The shoreline presents no easy access. It's
shin-deep muck near the water, edging a precipitous hillside of
extremely dense undergrowth, not unlike you would find in a
rain forest. At the exit of the tangled vines and twisted branches,
halfway up the embankment, there's another fifty feet of riprap,
loosely laid under tall grass and more brush. Perhaps the casino
is trying to create a defense against an assault from the river.

(Take-out below the hill near the casino)

On the bright side, the casino has a great buffet. I am seated where I can look out the skylight and see what is going on. It doesn't look good. A call home is made for a check on the weather radar. There is a major front of severe thunder storms approaching and it's not expected to pass until after 9:00. We check at the front desk and the lady says there are rooms available. The decision to cut the day short always comes hard but we're here and safe from the weather. There may not be another opportunity so convenient. The trek back to secure the boats and gather the stuff needed for the night is amidst a torrential rain.

"We made fifty-eight miles today and shouldn't lose sleep over it." We don't either. Luke is asleep a moment before his head hit the pillow or shortly after. I am a close second.

"One should count each day a separate life." -Lucius Annaeus Seneca, philosopher (BCE 3–65 CE)

Monday, June 1, 2008

At 5:00, we awake to the morning news and reports of winds in excess of 50 mph that swept through the area late yesterday, leaving a thousand people without electricity. Apparently, it was a wise decision not to go back on the river.

On the way to the boats, we talk about the stark contrast between this morning's 70 F and blue sky, and the cold wet mornings encountered on previous paddles.

Another fifty-one miles are behind us as we take a break on a small sand beach for a mid-afternoon lunch of Ramen soup, instant mashed potatoes, and dried beef. It's tough to beat a nutritious meal, a light breeze and summertime warm.

The rest of the afternoon passes with Luke listening to books on tape and me tuning into whatever radio station I can find. We try to connect during the hourly breaks, sometimes drifting nearly a mile in the allotted ten minutes. An hour before sundown, a brief break is taken across from the Great River Road State Park. It is extremely inviting but we need to make more miles due to the wind forecast for the next few days.

Paddling late is a risk we're willing to take. The high water has eliminated many of the normally abundant sand beaches, but not all of them. We keep paddling on, declining to stop at two more attractive sandbars.

With the sun well below the tree line and only a hint of twilight remaining, Luke sees a string of small trees near the center of the river; hopefully, it's an island. The sliver of moon scheduled to appear in another hour won't be of any assistance if this doesn't pan out. With eyes squinting in the darkness, we pick up the pace and make a new heading for the island. Yes! The kayaks run aground ten yards out from the beach. This piece of real estate, located three miles south of the confluence of the Arkansas and Mississippi rivers, was most likely under-water a month ago but provides a great campsite for tonight.

Holding our cell phones at arm's length above our heads, we have enough signal to get a message home that we are off the water and have made an outstanding eighty-seven miles today!

"It is pleasant to have been to a place the way a river went." -Henry David Thoreau, author and naturalist (1817–1862)

"Ka-Ka-Ska-Ska"

Tuesday, June 3, 2008

I awake early. An hour later when the sun appears, I give Luke notice that the day needs to begin. The wind was up before either of us. It's going to be a tough day so we waste no time getting on the river.

A midmorning two mile shortcut off the channel through a backwater saves time spent in the inexorable wind. The energy saved by not paddling against the wind balances out evenly with the extra energy exerted in the slower backwaters. Our spirits are better off having gotten out of the wind for awhile.

Speaking of spirits... Two miles east from where we take the shortcut, beyond the river, across the lowland, and on the other side of an oxbow known as Ferguson Lake, is the Winterville site complex consisting of flat-topped, rectangular ceremonial mounds of various sizes. Most of the mounds at the Winterville site were constructed during the Mississippian period, between 1200 and 1250 A.D. This intensive time of mound building reflects contact between local Indians of the Coles Creek culture and influences emanating from the great Cahokia site in Illinois, the largest mound center in the United States. Archeological excavations were conducted at Winterville in 1967–1968. The finds included structural remains, burials, and many ceramic and stone artifacts. The mounds are arranged around a forty-three acre plaza, at the center of which is the fifty-five foot high Mound A, the largest at the site. There are no extensive village remains, indicating that the site was occupied mainly during ceremonies. It is likely that only members of the social elite, such as chiefs, priests, and their retainers, were permanent residents of the site. Of the twenty-three mounds originally present, four were destroyed and several others reduced to remnants by agriculture and excessive grazing prior to the site's acquisition as a state park. Nevertheless, this mound group remains one of the largest and best-preserved in the southeastern United States. [10]

"The white men was many and we could not hold our own with them. We were like deer. They were like grizzly bears ... We were contented to let things remain as the Great Spirit made them. They were not, and would change the rivers ... if they did not suit them." -Chief Joseph of the Nez Perce (1840–1904)

Like yesterday – stopping only for a quick lunch – we carry on until all daylight has been consumed. Camp is on another narrow and not-so-level strip of sand where there's no cell signal tonight to call home and report our seventy-one miles.

Wednesday, June 4, 2008

The forecast is for the lower-nineties, a heat index of 97, more blue skies, and more wind – ramping up to 20–25 mph and gusts to 30 mph. Whitecaps and breaking waves are constant except for the reprieves when the river twists away from the wind. It's rough water all the way, especially when taking the outside corners of the main channel where the faster current hits slower water. The churning is similar to paddling in fast rapids with waves coming at you from almost every direction. It's plenty of fun, plenty of action and plenty of excitement. There are no close calls except for an encounter with a navigational-buoy-turned-kayak-magnet. Across from Mile Marker 471, I am paddling on river-right towards a green navigational buoy. I keep steering to the left but the current is drawing me to the right. Luke is a short distance behind and experiencing the same but, unlike me, is able to take the buoy on the inside. The current is unbelievably strong. No matter how hard I try to turn left, I remain zeroed in on the buoy. There is no other choice but, at the last minute, kick right and yield to the current and worry about getting straightened out after the buoy is behind. We pull it off again with a few yards short of taking a side trip. Later, a quick gawk at the map reveals this side channel that circumvents Island No. 97 is called Transylvania Chute. Of course, why wouldn't a channel guarded by a giant green kayak magnet have such a name? In hindsight, taking the chute may have been a fun little ride had we known for sure the channel re-entered the Mississippi in a timely manner. Soon after the bout with the buoy, there is a mighty nice sand beach where Luke and I take a lunch break. The GPS indicates an elevation of one hundred feet above sea level.

A mile downstream from our break, where Transylvania Chute returns to the Mississippi, the river gets wild. It is the craziest combination yet. The confluence of the rampant floodwaters in Transylvania Chute entering the Mississippi on an outside corner creates no less than three miles of solid Class III rapids. We hit speeds of 9 mph into the 25 mph headwind. (To anyone not on the scene, it would appear an exaggeration. For us who were there, however, it was a bona fide thrill ride.)

"As scarce as truth is, the supply has always been in excess of the demand." -Josh Billings, U S humorist (1818–1885)

It's a steady paddle throughout the afternoon as we lessen the distance to Vicksburg, the last Confederate-controlled section of the Mississippi River. Seven miles north of Vicksburg off Kings Point is where the ironclad ship U.S.S. Cairo gained fame on the cold morning of December 12, 1862 when it became the first ship in history to be sunk by an electrically detonated torpedo (actually an underwater mine). The Cairo was one of seven ironclad gunboats named in honor of towns along the upper Mississippi and Ohio rivers. These powerful ironclads were formidable vessels, each fitted with thirteen large cannons. Now on display in the Vicksburg National Military Park, the Cairo fought in only two other battles prior to meeting its fate – Plum Point in May and in the battle of Memphis in June. [11]

"We tend to overestimate the effect of a technology in the short run and underestimate the effect in the long run." -Roy Amara, engineer, futurist (1925–2007)

Sixty-eight miles downriver from where we slept last night, Luke and I set up camp in Room 419 at Diamond Jack's in Vicksburg. The buffet is featuring prime rib and seafood. After dinner, on the way back to the campground, I ask, "Do you ever think you'd want to do the whole trip again?"

"Absolutely, but for every momentary thought of how much fun it would be to do this entire trip again, there are a hundred fifty-two thoughts of *I never ever want to do this again!* Maybe, I'll feel differently after the memories of fighting against the wind fade."

"The Mississippi River in Minnesota begins by flowing north, then east, then south, then west and then southeast,

but the wind only blows in one direction: in your face." -Joe Angert, educator and canoeist

Thursday, June 5

As we ready the boats for take off, we make a pact, "There will be no more buffets, regardless how much spam, peanut butter and crackers are consumed throughout the day!"

The 7:45 start this morning is later than hoped for considering that the schedule calls for seventy miles of river before the next stop, Natchez.

The temperature is to get to 94 F which is ten degrees warmer than normal for this time of year, and it will be our third day of wind. According to the forecast, it should start tapering off late tomorrow. For now, it remains strong with gusts to 30 mph. The first thirty-five miles is the roughest water experienced throughout the day with a number of spots where waves easily stretch over the three-foot mark. The fast current is a blessing and, at times, speeds up to 9 mph are recorded on the GPS.

The highlight comes around 11:00 when approaching Grand Gulf Island Nuclear Power Plant. I am on river-right and Luke is on the other side of the river a half-mile away. I turn to check on Luke and see that he is talking to some guys in a small fishing boat. The conversation doesn't last long before the fishermen take off downstream and are not seen again.

I ask Luke about it at the next break. Luke said he was paddling along when all of a sudden a Jon boat came out of a side channel downriver and sped directly at him, cut the motor and pulled up alongside. There were five guys in the little craft but the driver did all the talking

"Hi. How's it going?"

"Good."

"Where did you start out today?"

"Vicksburg."

"Where are you going?"

"Gulf of Mexico."

"How long you been on the river?"

"Since last Saturday."

"Why you guys doing this?"

"We've been asking ourselves that same question."

They all laugh. The guys in the Jon boat give a wave good-bye and speed away.

Luke said there were several interesting things he noted. First, there was no fishing gear. Secondly, the driver was the only one with life a jacket that showed any wear. The others appeared relatively new. And third, there were a lot of empty beer cans tossed about in the bottom of the boat, but the two guys holding beer never took a drink. Take all this into consideration plus and the fact that they're out in the middle of nowhere, no landing, no houses, no towns, no nearby river access, and it's before noon on a beastly hot Thursday morning; it is very doubtful that this group of clean-shaven guys is anything else but Homeland Security poorly disguised as local Bubbas. "Ka-Ka-Ska-Ska." ("Busted!")

"If all mankind were suddenly to practice honesty, many thousands of people would be sure to starve." -G. C. Lichtenburg, scientist (1742–1799)

A storm front moves in after lunch, blackening the skies up-river, but only a few drops of rain fall on us. As the front moves on to the northeast, there's at least an hour of no wind. That changes twenty miles upriver from Natchez, once again making paddling more work than fun.

The city boat landing in Natchez does not appear to be a secure place to leave the kayaks so we paddle past the casino where we find a small beach and a nearby tree for the cable lock.

Resisting all temptation, Luke and I avoid the buffet and have the casino's shuttle driver take us directly to the Isle of Capri Hotel. Betty, a sweet little silver-haired lady in her seventies, is working the desk. "There you go. I gave you a room with a view of the river at no extra charge."

Luke, "We don't want it."

"What do you mean, you don't want it?"

"We don't want to look at the river." (Followed be the rest of the story.)

"You're crazy! You could get caught up in one of those whirlpool things and get sucked straight to the bottom. I have a friend who has one of those kayaks and I told her she better not let me catch her out on that river. And, if she ever did go out there and survived, I would beat her half to death when she got back."

"Simpletons! How long will you wallow in ignorance? Cynics! How long will you feed your cynicism? Idiots! How long will you refuse to learn?" -**Proverbs** 1:21 (The Message)

Friday, June 6, 2008

It's almost 9:00 before we leave Natchez, partly due to being tricked by the morning clerk who said, "Yes, there's a grocery store. Go to the light, turn left, go to the next light and it's on your right. It's no more than a few blocks." Reality: over a mile.

The other reason for the late start is finding my boat literally covered with ants. There were hundreds, maybe thousands, of the nasty little pests crawling all over the deck and inside everything. Not one ant on Luke's boat. The only explanation Luke can offer has something to do with clean living. "Ka-Ka-Ska-Ska." ("Yeah, right.") It takes a while to get all the gear cleaned up. For the rest of the day, no matter what twitch I feel down inside my boot, up my pant leg, under my lifejacket, or anywhere else, you know exactly what I was thinking.

"Ants never sleep." -Ralph Waldo Emerson, writer and philosopher (1803–1882)

According to the navigational maps, there are sand bars located sixty-three miles downriver. That will be the goal for today. As far as the weather goes, the temp is to hit 90 F by noon. Neither Luke nor I have much energy this morning. The day drags on without much dialogue, or anything exciting happening along the way. The wind is much less than it has been (18 mph with gusts to 23 mph) but the river is still fairly choppy, at least for the first twenty miles.

"To a crazy ship all winds are contrary." -George Herbert, Priest and poet (1593–1633)

We reach the area where the sandbars are supposed to be with an hour of daylight to spare. If the sandbars are present, they aren't to be seen tonight and must be under water. A bluff, on river-left over a couple of miles ahead and reflecting the low sun, may be an opportunity for camping. Luke and I paddle the hardest we have all day, trying to get to the bluff before sundown. With a thousand yards yet to go, I use my 8X monocular to check it out. No beach there. We don't want to, but it doesn't look like there's any other choice than to get ready to do some night paddling.

With so little light remaining, Luke believes he sees a sand point off to the right. Paddling hard again, we reach the opening in the trees, and once again are provided with a safe place until morning. As soon as the tents are pitched, I make a call home to report, "We made sixty-eight miles today and it looks like we'll have clear skies all night." Wrong again. A very brief thunderstorm passes through before 'lights out' at 9:30.

"One of the oldest human needs is having someone to wonder where you are when you don't come home at night."
-Margaret Mead, anthropologist (1901–1978)

Saturday, June 7, 2008

Baton Rouge, a major industrial, petrochemical, and port center of the American South, is the second largest city in Louisiana and the ninth largest port in the United States in terms of tonnage shipped. The fifty-eight mile distance to get there today shouldn't be a problem. All that remains of the wind is an occasional gentle and welcome breeze. Even though the drop in elevation between here and the Gulf is only seventy-five feet, the river is running strong and still creating a little crazy water in the outside corners.

But late in the day, we are cheated out of fast water on one corner. A southbound barge taking the corner too wide runs into shallow water, and a northbound barge coming up with a tender close behind forces us to the slow water on the inside. The eddy current makes for very difficult paddling. It's tough getting even 3 mph.

There is no landing at the casino, but there is a barge service area a hundred yards beyond that has a muddy beach bordering the casino parking lot. We drag the boats up, and walk back to the casino to get permission from security. Travis, the valet manager, gives the okay and is eager to assist us in finding lodging. The casino doesn't have any rooms, but he is willing to drive us to wherever we want to go. The problem is that we don't know where we want to go, so Travis along with us two smelly guys in the back of the limo drive from one place to the next looking for a room that will meet our budget. About fifteen miles east of the river somewhere – not sure where, Travis pulls up in front of the sixth hotel since leaving the casino and patiently says, "Check this one."

I hop out and go in. "It'll work." This place will always be referred to as the 'hotel in the hood.' A sign on the entrance door reads, "NO Refunds After 10 Minutes." The clerk sits behind bullet-proof glass, and between the hours of 9:00 P.M. and 7:00 A.M., an armed guard is on duty at the gate to the parking lot. Before leaving us, Travis gives me his business card and a telephone number to call in the morning for a ride back.

"Ka-Ka-Ska-Ska"

"Wherever there is a human being there is an opportunity for a kindness." -Seneca, Roman Stoic philosopher, statesman, dramatist (4BC-65AD)

Sunday, June 8, 2008

I am up at 4:30 to finish the laundry started the night before. Luke is out of bed an hour later. Not much after that, we call for the limousine. "It's on the way."

Making small talk with the driver, Luke tells him that we are looking forward to breakfast at the casino before moving on. The kid driving says that he has eaten there, and gives it a thumbs up.

Leaving our stuff with the valet, we go in search of breakfast. Not good... serving doesn't begin until 10:00.

Customer service people say, "The closest thing is a McDonalds two stop lights down the frontage road and then left. It's two blocks up the hill on the right."

A customer standing close by reiterates what the clerk has said and follows up with, "You can't miss it." We can, and do. It takes two hours to walk the six miles round trip to McDonalds.

"Fate is what happens to you when your luck runs out."
-Michael Garret Marino, author

As we leave the city, there is a lot of barge traffic – mostly tenders (smaller tows) that are positioning containers. One tender makes a deliberate crossing of the river directly at us, slows down, and over the PA speaker, a deep gentle voice says, "There are a number of thoughts going through my mind right now, but most of all I have a question about your sanity. You guys be sure to be careful out here and have a good trip." The response from the twosome is a simple wave and a smile.

Another captain further down the line says, "My, my, kay-aks on the mighty Mississippi." Others slow their engines and honk as Luke and I pass through the web of barges and tows. The courtesy shown to us kayakers invading their worksite was unexpected, but greatly appreciated. [Andy and Tony receive the same quality treatment when they paddle this section in the fall. They monitored the marine radio and listened as one captain would send word to the next on down the river about the kayakers in their midst.]

"The everyday kindness of the back roads more than makes up for the acts of greed in the headlines." -Charles Kuralt, journalist (1934–1997)

Lunch is in the shade of willow trees on a beautiful flat beach, but the time off the water is kept to under an hour even though our average moving speed is slightly over 6.0 mph.

Everything goes well for the next couple of hours, then the blue sky turns gray and it's obvious we are going to get wet. We're on a collision course with an isolated thunderstorm. The point of impact occurs in two-plus-foot waves on an outside corner, with no way to exit the river even if we wanted to. After the ten minute monsoon, Luke tells me that he wishes he could have had a video of what he looked like during the down-pour moments before, and what he saw from his vantage point, "Paddling hard, leaning into the wind-driven rain, squinting between the brim of my straw hat pulled down low and the glasses hanging on the end of my nose, my upper lip affixed over my lower lip to protect the cold sores from getting hit by the dime-sized liquid projectiles, taking the waves head on with the drenching spray breaking over the deck, and the bow of my boat rising high and slamming back down after each crest." He claims it would be no comparison to anything ever seen on the popular series, *Deadliest Catch* – probably not as dangerous, but just as exciting.

(Wave breaking over bow of barge)

Worried we won't find a good campsite downriver, we stop at 7:00 on a fantastic sand point that is flatter than Nebraska. Dinner is mashed potatoes and 'meat balls' (AKA dried beef) served with red wine, and chocolate pudding for dessert; meanwhile, we watch the sun sink below the trees on the distant shore setting the clouds ablaze in glory. It's a perfect place to be on a perfect evening.

"He gives his best; the sun to warm and the rain to nourish; to everyone, regardless: the good and bad, the nice and nasty." -Mathew 5:45 (The Message)

("He gives his best...")

Monday, June 9, 2008

We're on the water before 7:30 after a great night's rest. It's a bit humid, but the sky again starts out blue after an unbeatable overnight low of 72 F. There is very little wind and the flow of the river is good.

Forty miles is paddled before we stop for lunch in the early afternoon in the community of Wallace, LA. The decision is made easily because there is another front moving in. Up to this point, it looked like it would pass without incident, but when the thunder and lightning began, discussion ended.

"Ka-Ka-Ska-Ska"

Up over levee is a courthouse. There's a kid in the parking lot. "Is there any place close by, to either get a meal or something to snack on?"

"Yep. Go down this road, around the corner, and there's a convenience store on your left. It is less than a mile." Reality: two miles, one-way.

When you're on a paddle trip, you don't normally bring hiking shoes; consequently Luke has grown mammoth-sized blisters on his heals. People will often ask, "Don't your arms hurt when paddling long distances?" Ironically, your arms don't hurt. What hurts are your heels, from sitting on the bottom of the boat all day with nowhere to go. A foam pad helps, but provides little or no relief if your feet are rocking back and forth on blisters.

After a burger with the best part being the slice of onion, we walk back along the levee road to the courthouse where we take the opportunity to refill the water jugs. Before returning to the river, a brief conversation takes place with a very perceptive young man who recognizes kayakers when he sees them. The young man tells me, "The best fishing south of Minnesota is in the river passes near Venice, but be sure to watch out for bull sharks in that area."

"Ka-Ka-Ska-Ska." ("Good, something else to add to the list of creatures to be wary of.")

"Bull sharks are aggressive, common, and usually live near high-population areas like tropical shorelines. They are not bothered by brackish and freshwater, and even venture far inland via rivers and tributaries. Because of these characteristics, many experts consider bull sharks to be the most dangerous sharks in the world. Historically, they are joined by their more famous cousins, great whites and tiger sharks, as the three species most likely to attack humans."[12]

Jim Lewis

"Then God said, Let us make man in our image, in our likeness, and let them rule over the fish of the sea..."
-Genesis 1:26, The Bible NIV

The skies continue to be gray on the backside of the storm front, and the rain holds off a few hours as Luke and I paddle by the last of the sand beaches along the lower Mississippi. The absence of the sand beaches and safe places to camp is the reason why most people paddling the river down from the Headwaters end their voyage in New Orleans.

On day two of this trip, we decided to try to average sixty-four miles per day getting us to the Gulf in no more than a total of twelve days. By the time the rain begins to fall and twilight is upon us, we are on target with the twelve-day objective. There is a second objective, though. We want to position ourselves as close to New Orleans as possible tonight so we can get through the city early in the morning and have a jump on the heavy river traffic.

"New Orleans is the largest port in the United States and the third largest in the world. It is an extremely busy shipping terminal that handles vessels with drafts to forty feet as well as a multitude of smaller vessels engaged in a variety of marine transportation and service activities. River barge traffic is particularly evident as New Orleans is the southern terminus of the Mississippi River navigation system. The Port of New Orleans has more than one hundred eighty piers and wharves located on both sides of the Mississippi River, the Inner Harbor Navigation Canal, and the Mississippi River-Gulf Outlet Canal. There are over one hundred additional facilities for small vessels and barges located on adjacent waterways." [13]

"Ka-Ka-Ska-Ska"

There are miles of barges moored on river-left as we approach the north side of New Orleans this evening, still a good fifteen miles from downtown. The steady rain doesn't bother us or the locals fishing from shore on river-right. Luke says, "There is no way I am going to camp over there." Brian (in Memphis) had mentioned that the crime in this area is slightly higher than back home in Grand Rapids.

It's obvious we will not find a friendly spot for a tent on river-right, so we cross over in between a couple of northbound tows as the rain begins to slack off. On the other side, we continue on at a slower pace trying to locate anything that looks like it will work for us.

Now completely in the dark except for our headlamps and the work lights from the tows, we make our way along the moored barge containers. An ocean tanker passes by heading north. Downriver a quarter-mile, we can make out the line of flood lights on a dredge. We continue on past more parked barge containers and service tows. One of the guys working on a tow, looks down on Huck and Tom with uncertainty, "You guys alright?"

"Yes, we're fine." There's no point in asking about a campground — not while you're in an industrial park.

More workers on other barges stare in disbelief and give a wimpy wave as we paddle past in the darkness. A couple hundred yards beyond the dredge, there is an end to the long train of moored barges. It looks like a construction site above the sand bank. Luke goes in first to check it out and finds level ground where excavation has been going on. We'll be trespassing for sure, but it's not the first time. Rain gear is the first thing out of the hatch — not because it is raining, but it's needed for protection from the hoards of mosquitoes. Luke pitches his tent under a high voltage power line. It's too hot for the rain fly, so as he lay on his back looking up through the mesh, he finds himself staring directly at bright white flashing strobe. Across the river, the drone of diesel engines is in competition with the melodic sirens of the loading operation, adding a nice touch to the ambience of our 'campground.'

At 11:00, three hours after sunset, I am settled in, discussing the next day's strategy with Captain Morgan, while having a snack. A vehicle approaches and headlights illuminate the inside of my tent. Moments later, I hear the distinctive sound of the opening and closing of two doors on a pickup.

"God, please let it be security. No. No. God, please let it be friendly security."

Voice from outside the tent, "Can I help you?"

"Yes you can." I tell our story in the shortest and fastest version possible, adding a promise that we will on our way before sunrise.

"Sounds fine, just don't go near any of the excavating over in that direction. It could cave in."

"Thank you God."

Tonight is the first time I put this entire Mississippi River adventure into proper perspective. I am fifty-eight years old, been happily married for forty years, retired and financially comfortable, literally on the top of Maslow's Hierarchy of Needs Pyramid – lying here in a tent near midnight, smelling like a swamp in the middle of a construction site on private property, having not eaten since lunch, worrying about what lies ahead tomorrow as we paddle through the city. And to make matters worse, I'm confined to quarters because of the fog of mosquitoes lying in ambush outside. "This is truly insane."

"Ka-Ka-Ska-Ska"

"The closer one gets to the top, the more one finds there is no top." -Nancy Barcus, author

Tuesday, June 10, 2008

After a night with very little rest, we make the launch at dawn. As we begin to paddle, I discuss last night's reflection. Luke responds, "Look at it this way, we could be known as guys-who-sit-on-couch-a-lot."

"Yeah, let's get going."

(Waking up in New Orleans)

Twenty-two miles from where we camped last night, and with New Orleans now in the rearview mirror, Luke and I feel we have been duped by another myth. It's 8:30, and the only river traffic encountered this morning is one ocean tanker and a couple of barges. We even manage to avoid crossing paths with the two ferries that run almost continuously throughout the day.

"Don't tell me worrying doesn't help. Everything I worry about never happens." –Darlene Harris, Author's sister (1947-)

We stop for a late morning lunch in Belle Chase where the dude directing traffic at the ferry landing takes an interest in the kayaks. Luke asks him, "How far to the Gulf?" (Knowing it's seventy-six miles.)

"Maybe four or five hours in canoes like that."

Well, he must know much more about paddling than these two Minnesotans do because we don't expect to get there until late tomorrow afternoon.

Near 6:00, we have sixty-five miles in for the day. We stop on river-right in Woodland, another of the little communities along the river where people have made their home but only they know why.

Rudders are raised as we negotiate our way through sparse underbrush and over a wire fence barely sticking out of the calm water at the base of the levee. I offer to walk up over the levee to see what I can see and determine if it's worth dragging the boats up the forty-five degree concrete incline. At the summit, I look down into the backyards of a long row of manufactured trailer homes. It doesn't look like there are any services, only private dwellings, one of which isn't so private – two teenagers are in the backyard, playing a game of 'cuddle in the blanket.' I back away and report to Luke the results of my reconnaissance, "I doubt if there are any hotels here. At least, the couple I saw couldn't get a room."

"Be strong. Go back and ask them to make sure."

I muster all my might, and saunter back over the levee to find that the couple is still distracted by one another and still unaware of my presence. Two homes closer and out of view of the neighbor kids, however, a guy steps out on his back stoop and sits down to a plate of fried chicken.

I make the descent down the town-side of the levee wearing my green floppy hat and rust-red life jacket. My high black neoprene boots reach up to touch the bright red spray skirt flopping on my knees. The guy eating his supper hardly gives me more than a glance.

"I guess nothing that ever crawls over the levee would surprise you?"

"Nope."

"My friend and I are paddling down the river and wondering if there may be a hotel or campground in town within walking distance."

"Can't think of any near here. The closest hotel is in Empire... called Empire Inn."

"Is Empire on the river?"

"Yep."

"How far?"

"Ten miles."

"Okay, thank you."

"Good luck."

Returning to the river, Luke calls Traci for a telephone number for the Empire Inn, as he begins to backtrack his way to the main channel. I'm getting into my kayak.

"Jim, there's something over here that wasn't here when we came in."

"Is it a body?"

"No. But it does have a pair of eyes."

Luke finds another exit route from behind the undergrowth, while I paddle over to investigate. It's an alligator! (I don't discover until later that an alligator responds to splashing in the water as they feed, though they are normally timid around humans. An adult can exert over a thousand pounds of pressure with their jaws. On the plus side, there have been no known alligator attacks on kayaks.) I take a photo, and then another one appears, but it is more camera shy than his buddy.

(The gator)

The lady at the Inn tells Luke, "The hotel is right on the river. But to get to us, you have to take a channel off the river, go past the old bridge, and then stop at the landing before the new bridge."

"How will we know where the channel is located?"

"I don't know. I've never been there, but shrimp boats use it...We're real close to the new bridge. You can walk from there."

"Please keep a room for us. We'll be there at 8:30"

Full of new-found energy, we set a course for Empire, keeping our speed between 6.5–7 mph.

After almost twenty miles since reserving the room, the GPS indicates that the city of Empire is on river-right, but there is no side channel. Of course, it wouldn't easily be seen, though, because it's very dark out. It's blacker than the inside of a cow. We slow down and keep searching. An ocean tanker comes along side, out a couple hundred feet, stirring up three foot swells. Downriver is another boat, most likely a barge, that looks like it's running close to shore coming straight on. It has a lot more lights on it than the tanker that is running with hardly any. I wave my flashlight back and forth, and get a spot light in return from the boat out front. Good. Luke and I keep going, but not much faster than the current of the river. It doesn't appear that the boat or barge or whatever is coming toward us anymore, but has stopped along river's edge. The boat has more lights on it than any barge seen so far. Then it starts moving again – not up river, but off river. It could be the pass. We cautiously move up for a closer look, struggling to make out the details of the scene. There are so many bright lights from the boat, plus a number of other lights along both sides of the side channel – mostly red lights, and some are flashing. Luke says "Smell."

It's definitely shrimp. This must be the channel and that must be a shrimp boat. We're studying the situation, trying our best to give it definition, when the shrimp boat begins to sink right in front of us! "Oooh, this is a lock." We wait for the shrimp boat to get through the lock, and I radio lock tender. The response is static filled, so it is uncertain if the message actually got through. I radio again, and the gates open. We go in, go down, and exit out the other side. There to welcome us, in the shadows, is another alligator. The lady on the phone didn't mention that in the directions! A hundred yards beyond the old bridge, we see the new bridge and a boat landing just as described, right next to a hotel. As Luke and I drag the boats up the boat ramp, a half-dozen people appear on the balcony above and instantly begin with a barrage of questions. "What ya doing?" "Do ya need a room?" "Do ya'll need food? The grill is off, but we can get going again. Want a beer?"

"Is this the Empire Inn?"

"No, that's a mile up the road. Do ya need a ride there?"

"Ka-Ka-Ska-Ska." ("Let's see... a mile, uh? And how far is it using standards set by the International System of Units?") Actually, a side trip is taken with the car on our return from the Gulf. The one mile is in reality three miles, so it was a good decision to take a room here at the Delta Marina. Besides, you can't pass up a cold beer, especially when someone else is buying.

Wednesday, June 11, 2008

The restaurant doesn't open for another ninety minutes so I prepare oatmeal in the room before anything else is done to get ready. Soon after, while packing up the kayaks, a voice is heard from the balcony above, "Good morning. Come on up, I've got omelets ready for you guys." You can't pass up a free breakfast any more than you can say no to free beer. Sometimes, when a person begins to think, *It can't get any better than this.* – it does.

Before leaving, Luke and I try to pay for our room but are told not to worry about it.

"How much easier is it to be generous than just." –From the Letters of <u>Junius</u> collection (1772)

Twelve miles downriver from Empire is Fort Jackson, first occupied in 1832 after ten years of construction. Built in the shape of a pentagon, the red brick walls are twenty feet thick and the entire structure is surrounded by a moat. The foundation is made of cypress logs laid to level the fort in the swampy ground.

"In the 1840's it had been thought that Fort Jackson might be an important stronghold in the Mexican War, but it wasn't. Fort Jackson was then of only minor importance until the Civil War, when Louisiana seized the site for the Confederacy on January 8, 1861. The people of New Orleans felt safe knowing that Fort Jackson (and its sister fort, St. Philip, just to the east, on the other side of the river) were protecting them from the Union. Further, the mouth of the river had been obstructed with the wrecks of old ships and a heavy chain run from bank-to-bank. On April 18, 1862 USN Commander David D. Porter's armada began shelling Fort Jackson. The barrage continued all night and one of Porter's schooners was sunk. However, USN Flag Officer David G. Farragut's Western Gulf Blockading Squadron had been standing by and on April 20th breached Fort Jackson's outer obstructions. Yet it took until the early morning of April 24th for Farragut's ships to move past the two forts and fully engage the Confederate flotilla, eventually sinking or capturing thirteen vessels and breaking the back of the Confederacy's naval presence on the Mississippi.[14]

Jim Lewis

"To be prepared for War is one of the most effectual means of preserving peace." -George Washington, First President of the United States (1732–1799)

Under a sweltering sun, Luke and I reach The Jump at 1:00. It's ten minutes of paddling west, down the Grand Pass and another twenty snaking around on the Tiger Pass to get to the Venice Marina. Now it's time to play 'Let's make a deal.' Venice is the last road access on the Mississippi, and if we want to go to the end, it is going to have to either involve hiring a boat to bring us back upriver, or us paddling the eleven miles upstream in the heat of the day.

It's not easy to find someone willing to listen to the details of our request. These people are involved with a fishing tournament and they mean business. One thing turns to another and finally, I connect with a lady by the name of Diana Butler. She listens patiently to the story about the excursion down the big river, but her interest peaks when told that this last leg is being done as a fund raiser for the American Cancer Society. She immediately interrupts my rambling and says, "My two sons operate this marina. You stay here and I'll be right back."

She soon returns with her son, Mike. The story is repeated and Mike approaches a couple guys passing by on the dock with the proposal; each has his own excuse. It doesn't look good. There's a lot of hemming and hawing going on, so I tell Mike, "It's okay, we'll go to the Gulf via one of the side passes instead."

"No. You came this far, you are going to Mile Marker Zero! Exactly where and when do you need to have someone meet you?"

"It's 2:00 now. We'll need an hour to get back to the main channel and two more to get to the end. Let's say, 5:00 on river-right at the Head of the Passes, two and a half miles past Pilot-town (accessible only by water or helicopter)." I draw a map on a page from my notebook and hand it to Mike.

"How long are your kayaks?"

"This one is seventeen and that one's nineteen."

"Do you need a ride back to the main river channel?"

"No thanks, we'll be fine. Do you have an idea how much this is going to cost?"

"Don't worry, I've got it covered."

"We are all here on earth to help others; what on earth the others are here for I don't know." -W.<u>H</u>. Auden, poet (1907–1973)

Twenty minutes later, both of us are regretting we didn't take Mike up on the ride back to the main channel. Between the humidity, the heat, the dead calm air, and having to paddle up the current, this three mile section ranks with the most difficult paddling we have ever done. We reach the river in a little more than an hour, then turn south once more, and maintain a steady pace to the finish.

A crew boat is coming up from the gulf in the center of the channel at 4:59 when suddenly another smaller fishing boat swings out from behind it and heads directly at us. When we saw the crew boat coming, we swung outside of the navigational channel. Now we turn even more towards shore as the small craft keeps coming full speed. I'm thinking that we're going to have to do something quick. That's when the boat's throttle is cut and it drifts up to within a few feet of us. The guy aboard stands up and sticks his thumb out, and asks, "Need a lift?"

"Are you our ride?"

"Yes sir."

I check the GPS, "We have seven-tenths of a mile to go. Can you wait?"

"Not a problem."

At Mile Marker Zero, Captain Chris Calaway helps load the kayaks onto the deck of his twenty-four foot boat. He says he'll take it easy on the way back to the marina so as not to beat the kayaks up too badly.

It's 40 mph, and grins ear to ear all the way upstream back to the marina. "Ka-Ka-Ska-Ska." ("We did it!!!!")

Sharron arrives the next day and we three spend a night out on Bourbon Street celebrating. Luke flies home as scheduled and Sharron and I take our time over the next week to drive home.

(Luke McLeod)

(Jim Lewis, the author)

On November 6, 2008, Tony and Andy complete their journey down the Mississippi. I accompanied them on their thirteen day trip from Wilson to the Gulf, driving Tony's car and providing ground support along the way.

Jim Lewis

(Andy Albertson)

(Tony Shoberg)

"Ka-Ka-Ska-Ska"

Trip Report
 – 2,307.0 miles completed (100% of total trip)
 – 0 to The Gulf

Conclusion
"I heard somebody say the wealthiest place on earth is not Fort Knox or the oil fields of the Middle East. Nor is it the gold and diamond mines in South Africa. Ironically, the wealthiest places on earth are the cemeteries, because lying in those graves are all kinds of dreams and desires that will never be fulfilled. Buried beneath the ground are books that will never be written, businesses that will never be started, and relationships that will never be formed. Sadly, the incredible power of potential is lying in those graves." -Original Source unkown

I will not take dreams of paddling the Mississippi to my grave. I will take the memories. I will not lie on my deathbed wishing I would have captured the details on paper. I will smile knowing that the book was written; the story was told. I will not ever forget those who cheered us on, nor those along the way – for it is they who have made me strong. I have become rich!

And, if anyone ever tells me that they are planning to paddle the entire Mississippi, my response will be "Ka-Ka-Ska-Ska." ("What??!! Are you crazy??!!")

"The first river you paddle runs through the rest of your life. It bubbles up in pools and eddies to remind you who you are." -Lynn Noel, **Voyages: Canada's Heritage Rivers**

Jim Lewis

References:

1) "The Mighty Mississippi River"
   http://users.stlcc.edu/jangert/index.html)
2) "Native American History in the Mississippi Headwaters Region"
   http://www.mvp.usace.army.mil/docs/history/nativeamerican.pdf
3) Mississippi Headwaters Board
   http://www.mhbriverwatch.dst.mn.us
4) Minnesota Department of Natural Resources
   http://www.dnr.state.mn.us
5) "Frostbite: The cold, hard facts"
   http://www.emslive.com
6) "Muscatine, IA"
   http://en.wikipedia.org/wiki/Muscatine,_Iowa
7) "History of Montrose"
   http://www.montroseia.us/
8) "St. Louis, Missouri"
   http://en.wikipedia.org/wiki/St_Louis_(MO)
9) "Monarch Butterfly – North America's Migrating Insect"
   http://www.fs.fed.us/monarchbutterfly/migration/index.shtml
10) "Winterville Site"
    http://www.nps.gov/history/nr/travel/mounds/win.htm
11) "U.S.S. Cairo Gunboat"
    http://www.nps.gov/vick/u-s-s-cairo-gunboat.htm
12) "Bull Shark"
    http://animals.nationalgeographic.com/animals/fish.htm
13) "Port of New Orleans"
    http://www.globalsecurity.org/military/facility/new-orleans-port.htm

14) "City of Dust"
http://cityofdust.blogspot.com/2005/10/fort-jackson-louisiana.html

15) "U.S.S. Cairo Gunboat"
http://www.nps.gov/vick/u-s-s-cairo-gunboat.htm

Photos by:
1) Andy Albertson
2) Brian Smith
3) Jim Lewis
4) Luke McLeod
5) Tony Shoberg

Made in the USA
San Bernardino, CA
29 April 2016